Praise for *UX for Lean Startups*

"A must read to find Product Market fit."

Andy Rachleff—President and CEO, Wealthfront;
Cofounder, Benchmark Capital

"Laura is an expert at teaching entrepreneurs how to understand their users and design innovative products. This book should be required reading for anybody with a startup."

Brett Durrett—CEO, IMVU

"Building great products starts with deep customer understanding, which is surprisingly hard to attain. In this book, Laura walks you through the nuts and bolts of learning from customers and shows you how to turn this learning into an amazing product."

Ash Maurya—Founder, USERcycle

"Making products that people buy, use, and love is a whole lot easier if you know Laura Klein's brilliant, no-nonsense Lean UX tools and tricks. She is an expert practitioner with a wealth of knowledge accumulated from years of working in Lean Startups and evolving the art of Lean UX. This book is an invaluable contribution to our field."

Joshua Kerievsky—CEO, Industrial Logic, Inc.

"I expect you to put this book down a lot. Not because it's bad; quite the contrary—it's funny, readable, and dare I say charming. It's just that there are so many good ideas and five-minute epiphanies within its covers, you won't be able to resist constantly firing off an email or picking up a pen and trying stuff out as you read it."

Alistair Croll—Founder, Solve For Interesting

UX for Lean Startups

Faster, Smarter User Experience Research and Design

Laura Klein

O'REILLY®

Beijing · Cambridge · Farnham · Köln · Sebastopol · Tokyo

UX for Lean Startups

by Laura Klein

Published by O'Reilly Media, Inc., 1005 Gravenstein Highway North, Sebastopol, CA 95472.

O'Reilly books may be purchased for educational, business, or sales promotional use. Online editions are also available for most titles (safari.oreilly.com). For more information, contact our corporate/institutional sales department: (800) 998-9938 or corporate@oreilly.com.

Editor: Mary Treseler
Production Editor: Kara Ebrahim
Copyeditor: Kiel Van Horn
Proofreader: Julie Van Keuren
Indexer: Angela Howard

Cover Designer: Mark Paglietti
Interior Designers: Ron Bilodeau and Monica Kamsvaag
Illustrator: Kara Ebrahim
Compositor: Holly Bauer

May 2013: First Edition.

Revision History for the First Edition:

2013-04-24	First release
2013-09-06	Second release

See *http://oreilly.com/catalog/errata.csp?isbn=0636920026242* for release details.

ISBN: 978-1-449-33491-8
[CW]

Contents

Foreword

This book will make you a better designer. If you're already a designer, that probably sounds pretty good. But I believe this is true for just about anyone, from engineers to MBAs.

I have had the privilege of working with Laura Klein for many years. She is a fantastic designer and has worked on many outstanding products. (Don't tell her I said this, but she's also a pretty good programmer, too.) But her talents as an individual contributor are surpassed by her ability to impact whole teams. And I am pleased to report that this extremely rare skill has now been translated into book form.

Laura has a special talent for helping nondesigners access the arcane toolkit that is sometimes called interaction design, usability testing, user experience (UX) design, or—as is my preference—making things that work. Whatever you call it, every modern company must realize that good design drives growth, customer satisfaction, and continuous innovation. This book will put those tools immediately in your hands, no matter what it says on your business card.

Startups require good design, but they can't always afford a full-time designer. In fact, many of the most famous startups had nobody on staff trained in traditional design. Unfortunately, the kind of rapid, cross-functional collaboration that startups require is often at odds with the traditional approaches most designers grew up with. So in order to take advantage of the strengths of the design discipline, we need new approaches that support speed, collaboration, and experimentation.

If you're reading this, chances are you work in a startup or hope to become an entrepreneur someday. But one of the most important things we in the Lean Startup movement have been evangelizing is that anyone who is trying to create something new under conditions of high uncertainty is an entrepreneur—no matter what their job description. If you find yourself becoming an "involuntary entrepreneur"—for example, someone inside an established company who faces high uncertainty all of the sudden—you will find these tools especially useful.

If you're looking for a book of abstract theory, aesthetic jargon, or gentle clichés, look elsewhere. This is simply the most practical design book, ever. It pulls no punches and accepts no excuses. Complicated concepts like the Minimum Viable Product are made accessible: it's a cupcake, not a half-baked bowl of ingredients (see pages 138–139). And every chapter is loaded with step-by-step instructions for how to make each concept come to life.

But by far my favorite part of this book is that every tip, every concept, every tool, every approach is placed in its proper context. It is extremely rare to see any expert—let alone a designer—explicitly tell you when not to use their "best practices." But in real life, there is no such thing as a best practice. Every practice is contextual. Used in the wrong situation, every tool can become extremely harmful. Every tool and recommendation in this book (except one, which I leave as an exercise to the reader to find) comes with an explanation of when to skip it; most are helpfully labeled with their own "When is it Safe to Skip This?" headings.

Laura and I worked together long before I wrote the book *The Lean Startup: How Today's Entrepreneurs Use Continuous Innovation to Create Radically Successful Businesses*. I still cringe when reading some of the highly entertaining stories Laura tells of failed products and bad decisions; many of those mistakes were made by me. Let my dumb mistakes be your gain: listen to Laura Klein and do what she says. Become a better designer. Build great products. Make your customers' lives better.

Good luck.

Eric Ries
San Francisco, CA
April 15, 2013

Preface

Who Should Read This Book

This book is for entrepreneurs. It's also for product designers, owners, and managers who want to make products that people will buy, use, and love. It's especially for people who are creating products in startups or companies that are trying to innovate like startups.

Don't worry if you're not a designer. It doesn't matter if you've never made a wireframe or talked to a user. If you read this book, you're going to learn enough about user experience (UX) to let you design your own product. No prior background in user experience or any other type of design is necessary to understand the concepts in this book.

This book is for decision makers. This book won't teach you how to sell your idea to your manager or how to convince people that user research is helpful or that a good user experience is necessary. What it will do is give you specific tools and tips for learning, designing, and shipping something amazing.

You see, this book is only for people who want to build things. Right now. It's for people who want to learn how to make products that people will love without wasting a lot of time and money.

Like I said, this book is for entrepreneurs.

What Is This Book About?

Fantastic user experiences are becoming a requirement for new products. Unfortunately, if you've ever tried to build one, you'll know that fantastic user experiences are incredibly hard to deliver. It's even harder when you're building something new and innovative.

In fact, one of the only things harder than building an intuitive, delightful, innovative, easy-to-use product is hiring a designer to do it for you.

This book was written to help you create a fantastic user experience for your product. It will teach you how to understand your user in order to build something brand new that people will love and possibly even pay you for (if that's what you're into).

While focusing on UX design techniques and processes, I'm also going to cover a bit about Lean Startup, a methodology created and popularized by Eric Ries. Perhaps you've read his book, *The Lean Startup* (Crown Business)? It's really good, but don't worry if you haven't read it. It's not a prerequisite.

This book will make a lot of references to web-based products and software, but the UX design techniques in this book will work equally well for building most things that have a user interface. Hardware, software, doorknobs...if you sell it and people interact with it, then you can use Lean UX to better understand your customers and to create a better product faster and with less waste.

How to Use This Book

My editor wanted me to write a section explaining how to use this book. My first draft just said, "Read it," but apparently that wasn't specific enough, so I've written a couple of tips for getting the most out of the book.

You don't have to read this book in order. It's designed so that you can skip around, find something that's pertinent to you in your current product development cycle, and learn an important tip about making your product better or your process faster. I don't expect you to sit down and read it cover to cover before starting your company. Who's got that kind of time?

Although you don't have to read it all the way through, there are parts you may want to read a few times. You see, there are going to be things in the book that sound easy, but really they require quite a lot of practice. All the user research stuff, for example, is a bit harder than it sounds. It's nice to have a book like this around for reference when things get tough. Also, my name is right on the cover, so it's handy when you want to swear at me for making something sound easier than it is.

Even if you do read it cover to cover, don't feel like you have to do everything in the order I present it. There's no exact recipe to follow that will get you to a fantastic product. Sometimes you need to design, sometimes you need to observe users, sometimes you need to run tests, and sometimes you need to do all that and a few dozen other things at the same time. In this book, you will learn practical, hands-on tactics for doing all those things leaner, better, faster, and more cheaply.

And if you're still confused about how to use the book, I will point out that it also makes a great paperweight, doorstop, and holiday gift. Do not eat this book.

If you're still confused about how to use this book or about any of the information in it, you can always reach me at *laura@usersknow.com*.

We'd Like to Hear from You

Please address comments and questions concerning this book to the publisher:

O'Reilly Media, Inc.

1005 Gravenstein Highway North

Sebastopol, CA 95472

(800) 998-9938 (in the United States or Canada)

(707) 829-0515 (international or local)

(707) 829-0104 (fax)

We have a web page for this book where we list errata, examples, and any additional information. You can access this page at:

http://oreil.ly/ux-lean

To comment or ask technical questions about this book, send email to:

bookquestions@oreilly.com

For more information about our books, courses, conferences, and news, see our website at *http://www.oreilly.com*.

Find us on Facebook: *http://facebook.com/oreilly*

Follow us on Twitter: *http://twitter.com/oreillymedia*

Watch us on YouTube: *http://www.youtube.com/oreillymedia*

Safari® Books Online

Safari Books Online (*www.safaribooksonline.com*) is an on-demand digital library that delivers expert content in both book and video form from the world's leading authors in technology and business.

Technology professionals, software developers, web designers, and business and creative professionals use Safari Books Online as their primary resource for research, problem solving, learning, and certification training.

Safari Books Online offers a range of product mixes and pricing programs for organizations, government agencies, and individuals. Subscribers have access to thousands of books, training videos, and prepublication manuscripts in one fully searchable database from publishers like O'Reilly Media, Prentice Hall Professional, Addison-Wesley Professional, Microsoft Press, Sams, Que, Peachpit Press, Focal Press, Cisco Press, John Wiley & Sons, Syngress, Morgan Kaufmann, IBM Redbooks, Packt, Adobe Press, FT Press, Apress, Manning, New Riders, McGraw-Hill, Jones & Bartlett, Course Technology, and dozens more. For more information about Safari Books Online, please visit us online.

Acknowledgments

Books don't write themselves (unfortunately), and anybody who thinks the author is the only one responsible for the writing is completely delusional. In other words, there are a whole lot of people I would like to thank for helping me turn a bunch of ideas into something that people might want to read.

First, I'm pretty sure I'm contractually obligated to thank Eric Ries for getting this whole crazy Lean thing started. He is fantastic, and I owe him more than I could ever repay.

I also want to thank everybody at O'Reilly for being generally amazing, but also specifically for answering all of my stupid questions and putting up with my bizarre unicorn-related requests. Mary, Nathan, Kara, and Kiel, you are saints.

I'd like to say thanks to Eric Prestemon for all of his love and encouragement. I never would have started writing the blog if Eric hadn't said, "Will you please stop talking about this stuff and just write it all down?" I love you, honey, even though you don't want to listen to me complain about UX all the time.

Thank you as well to everyone else who contributed to this book—all the people who read it early and gave great feedback and said nice things about it in public. You are wonderful. Thank you especially to Sarah Milstein for reassuring me that I could finish this thing, even at my darkest moments.

I couldn't have done any of this without Ellen and Julie at Sliced Bread Design. They are the people who turned me into a UX designer in the first place. Thanks for taking a chance on me.

And, of course, I owe the biggest thank you to Marianne and Tony Klein for...well...everything, really. I love you both. It's the future.

Introduction

I'm a little tired of the phrase "Get out of the building."

Don't get me wrong. It's a wildly important concept. If you're not familiar with Steve Blank and Eric Ries and the whole Lean Startup methodology, you should be. It's good stuff.

Steve and Eric talk a lot about getting out of the building, and there's an excellent reason for that. Getting out of the building is a great way to make products that people want to buy. Sadly, sometimes it's easier to understand the importance of something than it is to put it into practice.

Of course, the goal of getting out of the building is to get you in better touch with your users. If you have a question about how your product should work or what feature you should build next, the answer is not in that airless conference room you're trapped in. It's not on the whiteboard. It's not the result of an endless brainstorming session with other people at your company. Even your CEO does not have the answer.

Your answer is somewhere in the world outside the building, and your customers can help you find it. You just need to know how to learn from them. This is one of the most important concepts of Lean Startup. You need to validate things with your customers early and often in order to keep learning. If you missed that part of Eric and Steve's work, you should take another look. It's kind of a big deal.

If you've been paying attention to the rest of the talk about Lean Startup, then you've heard that user experience is also incredibly important. You have to know how to design simple things, A/B test them, and then iterate.

Oh, and don't forget continuous deployment, Agile development, and Minimum Viable Products.

Of course, if you've ever tried to do any of those things, you've probably figured out that they can all be ridiculously hard to do.

Take "getting out of the building" as an example. Did you realize that there's a whole industry built around this? There are huge numbers of people who have studied this in school and who do this professionally. These people are often called things like "user researchers," and they know all sorts of things about what kind of research to do and when and how to get the right sort of information from people. They figure out what's wrong with your product and explain what you need to do to fix it. And they charge you a lot of money for it.

The same goes for user experience design. There are people who have been designing products for years. They've studied great designs and terrible ones. They've spent their careers trying to design things simple enough for people to understand and delightful enough for people to want to use.

Unfortunately, there is a terrible shortage of these types of people, so it's very likely that you're trying to build a product without one. Or maybe you were lucky enough to find a designer, but she's mostly good at visual design or she's never worked in anything other than a waterfall environment. Or you might even be a designer or user researcher, but you've never worked in the terribly chaotic and insane world that is a new startup.

As one of the above-mentioned types of people, you're now being told that you need to get out of the building; and to design a responsive, elegant, simple interface; and to do it all agilely; and could you also raise a few million dollars and hire a bunch of rockstar engineers and...your old job with a steady paycheck and weekends off is starting to look pretty good right about now, isn't it?

So why am I telling you all of this? You know how hard it is. You don't need me going on and on about it.

Here's the deal. I'm going to assume that you've already learned how hard all this can be. I'm going to make it easier for you.

Instead of pontificating about how important design is or giving you marginally relevant examples of how other companies did things, I'm just going to give you some tools to help you get out of the building, design a simple product, and validate all your assumptions. I won't make you an expert, but I'll teach you some useful tricks so that you can build a better product. Maybe, with a little practice, you'll be able to build something that people actually want to use.

I'll even throw in a few tips about how to measure your successes and failures so that you don't keep doing the same stupid things over and over and over. Think how much time that will save.

So welcome to the world outside the building. Let me show you where to go next.

What Is Lean UX, Anyway?

Lean UX is more than a buzzword. In some ways, it's a fundamental change in the way we design products. In another way, it's a bunch of stuff that a lot of us have been doing for a long time.

In fact, a lot of people who have been doing user-centered design or Agile design are confused by what all the fuss is about Lean UX. There's a reason for that. A lot of Lean UX is going to seem very familiar to people who are used to Agile design and user-centered design.

But Lean UX also introduces a few new things that aren't found in other design practices. It takes many of the best parts of the design practices that have come before it, and it adds its own twist. Let's look at the things that define Lean User Experience Design.

Lean UX Is About Validating Hypotheses

Much like the rest of Lean Startup, Lean UX centers around validating hypotheses. This is quite a departure from traditional design, which often revolves around fulfilling a designer or product owner's "vision."

Instead of thinking of a product as a series of features to be built, Lean UX looks at a product as a set of hypotheses to be validated. In other words, we don't assume that we know what the user wants. We do customer interviews and research in order to develop a hypothesis about what a customer might want, and then we test that hypothesis in various ways to see if we were right. And we keep doing that every time we make a change to the product.

Let's look at an example before and after applying Lean UX practices.

Before Lean UX, Company X might have said, "We need to record user comments for each product and display them on the product page." The product manager would have spent time writing a spec for comments on product pages. A designer might have come in and designed a great comment experience. Engineers would then have written code that matched the spec and the design. The whole process might have taken two or three months.

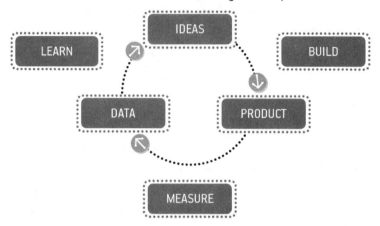

Figure I-1. The Lean loop

At the end of the process, the product pages would allow users to leave comments. But so what? Would this make users spend more money on products? Would they stick around for longer? Would users even bother to leave comments? What is the actual benefit to the company for spending those three months on building a comment system rather than on something else?

The problem with this approach is that it starts with a feature rather than a hypothesis. It assumes that comments on product pages are necessary rather than identifying a user problem, coming up with an idea that might solve that user problem, and designing a test to see if the idea is true.

Here's a leaner way to approach the problem.

Let's say that, instead of deciding that comments are necessary, Company X says, "We need to find a way to improve our revenue. Based on our preliminary research, we believe that allowing users to leave comments on product pages will cause customers to become more engaged and buy more items. How can we figure out if that's true?"

Now this has been restated in a way that allows the company to validate the hypothesis and easily change the feature if it turns out to be the wrong way to improve the metric.

Once Company X has a hypothesis—that adding comments will increase revenue—the Lean User Experience Designer could figure out the best way to validate or invalidate that hypothesis. That might be something as simple as gathering some comments from users about products and adding those comments to the page manually to see if having comments on the page affects whether users buy more products.

Could the result still be adding a feature that enables user comments on product pages? Sure! The difference is that you will know whether this is the right feature to build long before you spend a lot of time and money building it. You'll also be able to get some great customer feedback on exactly how the feature should work, so you don't have to go back and fix it later.

Lean UX isn't about adding features to a product. It's about figuring out which metrics drive a business, understanding what customer problems we can solve to improve those metrics, generating ideas for fixing those customer problems, and then validating whether or not we were correct.

If that all seems rather daunting, don't worry. I'll share some very specific methods for doing this later in the book.

But It's Not Just About Validating Hypotheses...

I was speaking with one startup, and they explained that they had done a small test of a particular new feature and measured their conversion funnel. About 3% of people had converted to using the feature. Unfortunately, they had no way to tell whether 3% conversion was a fantastic outcome or a complete failure because nobody had ever built this sort of feature before.

This is a trap I see a lot of Lean startups fall into: the inability to interpret whether or not a hypothesis has been validated.

Of course, when possible, Lean User Experience Design encourages designers to A/B test their changes, and A/B tests are typically quite easy to interpret—either a change makes a statistically significant difference or it doesn't. I'll have lots more on this later in the book. However, there are other types of tests to run, and they aren't always as easy to interpret as a straight A/B test.

Sometimes, when you're trying to validate hypotheses in new industries, it can be tough to know what sort of results constitute a success. With Lean UX, you must learn how to design the right kinds of tests in order to know when your hypotheses have been validated. And sometimes you just have to rely on plain old qualitative research and good judgment. We'll cover that in later chapters.

Lean UX Is User Centered

I can't tell you how often I've talked to designers who are trained in User-Centered Design (UCD) and they've told me, "Oh, you're prototyping and talking to users? I do that! I must be doing Lean UX!"

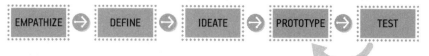

Figure I-2. All of these things are used in both UCD and Lean UX

And that's partially true. Lean UX borrows heavily from UCD, largely because UCD is awesome. For example, Lean Startup didn't come up with the idea of learning from users. Hell, some of us have been doing that for decades, and we learned from people who had been doing it even longer.

This is great, because it means that getting product feedback is not a new science. Lean teams don't have to figure out how to learn from users on their own. There are lots of people practicing UCD and doing user research who can help guide them. In fact, if you want to learn to be a fabulous Lean User Experience Designer, you could do a lot worse than starting by getting a good grounding in User-Centered Design.

But It's Not Just About User-Centered Design...

Whenever my UCD friends say they're doing Lean UX because they make interactive prototypes or run usability studies, I have to correct them.

Lean UX does borrow very heavily from UCD, but it also adds many of its own flourishes. For example, UCD doesn't really have a strong opinion about things like frequent iterations, validating hypotheses, or Agile teams. Lean does. UCD also doesn't have any concept of measuring design outcomes in a scientific manner, while that is central to the Lean methodology.

Don't think of Lean UX as something that is replacing UCD or that is better or worse than UCD. It's a set of tools that includes much of what is so wonderful about User-Centered Design—mainly its relentless focus on the user.

I'm not going to teach you to be a fantastic User-Centered Designer in this book, but hopefully I'll show you enough tricks to get your product off the ground and teach you how to incorporate great User-Centered Design into your process.

Lean UX Is Agile

After there was User-Centered Design, there was Agile Design. And Lean UX steals a lot of great stuff from Agile, too.

For example, Agile Design includes cross-functional teams where designers and developers work directly together on a project rather than treating the design department as an external agency. The cross-functional team is critical to Lean UX. By including developers, designers, and product owners in the majority of decisions, it makes the entire design process faster and easier to change when things aren't going well.

Agile gets rid of a lot of documentation and specifications in order to be more...well, agile. Lean also eschews a lot of traditional documentation. Instead of always creating a PRD and a pixel-perfect mockup of every screen, both Lean and Agile concentrate on providing the type of documentation that is most useful for communicating design to the team. Why write a 300-page Word document when a flow diagram or a sketch will do the trick?

Perhaps most importantly, both Agile Design and Lean UX get rid of the waterfall methodology of the past where research and design could take months or even years before getting delivered to engineering as a "final spec," which was often wrong.

Like Agile, Lean focuses on working quickly and in short cycles in order to reduce the amount of time until the team gets feedback on the product.

But It's Not Just About Being Agile...

While Lean UX takes a huge number of best practices from Agile Design, that's not the whole story.

Lean replaces traditional user stories that can be declared "done" by a product owner with User Hypotheses that can be validated or invalidated. In other words, a feature isn't finished when it's shipped to a user. A feature is often simply a method of validating whether allowing a new customer behavior is good or bad for the business.

When working in Agile Design environments, I would often be asked to check a feature in a staging environment in order to determine if it was finished and could be accepted. In Lean UX, that question can't be answered until the feature has been used by customers and the results on key metrics have been measured. And even then, the feature isn't really "finished." It's just ready for its next iteration.

It may seem like a small distinction, but the concept of measuring design output is something that has the potential to dramatically change the product design industry for the better. Unsurprisingly, I'll cover measuring design in much more detail in later chapters.

Lean UX Is Data Driven

Speaking of data, Lean UX is solidly data driven.

One of the most important ideas behind Lean UX is that we don't assume that a new design or feature is automatically better than what came before it. We test everything. When we ship a new feature, we test to see if it made a significant impact on important user behaviors. When we change text or the timing of an email, we test to see which version performs better. When we make a change to a user flow or a navigational structure, we make sure we haven't inadvertently made things worse for users.

Even more importantly, we use this deploy-and-test process as a feedback loop for the designers. If we made a change that we fully expected to improve things, but it actually hurt key metrics, we use that as a basis to investigate what went wrong. Which assumptions were made that were incorrect? Which hypotheses have been invalidated?

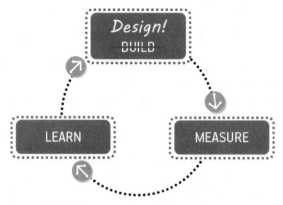

Figure I-3. You can't learn if you don't measure

By testing every iteration of a feature's design, we help the designer learn more about real user behavior. We also have specific metrics that we can use to show the return on investment for design projects.

This is something that is unique to Lean UX, in my experience. Of course, designers and user researchers have been running qualitative usability tests on their products for many, many years, but this sort of quantitative measurement of the actual effect of specific design changes on shipped products was not widespread until recently, especially not at startups.

Some members of the design community have also resisted it quite vigorously because they feel that "design can't be measured" or that somehow quantifying the impact of design detracts from the purity of the process. This, in my opinion, is utter bullshit.

The way something is designed can either improve a product's usability and desirability or destroy it. It is in our best interest, as designers and product owners, to measure the real impact that our work has on the bottom line of our products and companies. But don't worry. We can fight about this later in the book.

But It's Not Just About Data...

One fairly common argument against Lean UX is that somehow all this data is removing the vision from the craft. This may be the root of why many designers are so resistant to the idea of data-driven design. They've heard about Google testing 41 shades of blue, and they think that all design will be reduced to this sort of "just test everything" approach.

This couldn't be further from the truth. While it's true that things like picking the best color for links is something that is easily done with a multivariate test, it's also true that real design changes, not just tiny optimizations, are made by designers and people with vision and passion for a product.

Just because we are testing how our changes affect the bottom line of the product doesn't mean that we're not making the critical design decisions. Instead of thinking of Lean design as being driven by data, you can think of it as being informed by data. Data can tell us things like what people are doing and where people are falling out of funnels, but only good research and design will tell us why that's happening and how to fix it.

Data-driven design isn't about simply trying everything you can think of and picking the things that convert best. It's about combining good design practices with good testing practices in order to create a more successful product. If you're not convinced yet, I'll go into the right and wrong way to test designs later in the book.

Lean UX Is Fast and Cheap (Sometimes)

Lean often gets misunderstood as a synonym for "as cheap as possible." This simply isn't true. Lean Startup, like Lean UX, has nothing to do with whether a company is bootstrapped or Fortune 500. A Lean Startup does not mean a cheap startup. It never has.

However, I have found that Lean UX is frequently faster and cheaper than traditional UX, almost entirely because Lean UX strives to eliminate waste.

Imagine for a moment how much it costs to do a full round of traditional user research followed by a month or two of design and usability testing before writing a line of code. I don't actually have to imagine that. I worked at an agency that did that sort of work, and the answer is easily in the tens of thousands of dollars, and sometimes significantly more. Remember, that's before you've validated your initial product idea at all.

Now, imagine that you do all that work, but after you launch your product nobody buys it, because nobody particularly likes your idea.

For example, perhaps you've heard of a company called Webvan. They spent somewhere in the neighborhood of $400 million building an automated warehouse system just to figure out that people weren't yet ready to shop for groceries online.

Instead of building before you validate, imagine that you start with a few lightweight experiments to test your product hypothesis, realize that it's absolutely wrong and that nobody will pay for it, and keep iterating and pivoting until you find something that people are interested in buying.

For example, instead of building an entire infrastructure capable of delivering groceries to millions of people, Webvan could have experimented with a static website, a limited range of products, and a concierge service. Or they could have started out by partnering with stores that already sold groceries. In fact, if they'd started out that way, they might have been able to save enough money to survive until people were ready to get all their groceries delivered.

Either way, they would have avoided spending a lot of time and money on building something nobody wanted in favor of spending a little time and money finding something people might pay them for.

I'm no economist, but I'd say that the second version of that story is a whole lot cheaper than the first one. And that's the point, really. Lean UX saves you time and money not because you're refusing to invest in good design. Lean UX saves you money by keeping you from spending lots of time and money on stuff nobody wants.

Lean UX still requires a solid investment in the tools and people necessary to do good design. It just keeps them from designing the wrong things.

But It's Not Just About Being Cheap and Fast...

Lean UX is not bad UX, and building a good user experience is not cheap. You can't refuse to spend any money on research and design and then say you're being Lean. You're not. You're being stupid.

In this book, I'm going to provide you with a lot of tips that will help you move faster and get better results with less waste. But I'm not going to tell you how to design a fabulous product for free, because that's just not possible.

Design and research still take time and money to do correctly. But by spending your time and money wisely, at least you'll wind up with a great product that people want to use. The rest of this book will teach you how to do your research and design with less waste and how to learn the right things at the right time.

Lean UX Is Iterative (Always)

A huge part of Lean UX involves something called the Minimum Viable Product (MVP), which I'm going to talk about at length later on in the book. It gets its own chapter! The short version of the MVP definition is that you're going to build the smallest possible thing you can in order to conclusively validate or invalidate a hypothesis.

There is a very, very important concept that many people seem to miss, however. Once you've created an MVP, you need to keep working on it. You see, if everything is a hypothesis that you need to validate, then once you've validated that hypothesis, you need to act on it.

Lean UX is all about gathering actionable metrics. Of course, the key to being successful with actionable metrics is that you must do something with them. They're not something that just make you feel good about yourself. They are important tools for deciding what to do next.

What this creates is an incredibly iterative process, where you're constantly building small things, learning from them, and then continuing to build—or occasionally destroy—based on what you've learned.

To keep the cycle going, you must keep iterating and building. I have seen too many bad Lean Startups with products that are littered with abandoned or half-built features. Their intentions were good. They were trying a lot of different things but then just leaving them to rot.

Trying new things constantly and then abandoning them without further study or work is not iterating. That's flailing. And, more importantly, it's what leads to wildly overcomplicated products with a weird mix of abandoned features used by a small percentage of users.

One startup I worked with had no fewer than three different ways to search its site at one time. Instead of iterating on the first version, it kept creating new versions of search with slightly different features, leading to one of the most confusing experiences I've ever seen for users who just wanted to search for a product. I'll talk about ways to avoid this sort of problem throughout the book.

With Lean UX, you need to constantly be improving your product, not just by adding new features, but also by improving the experience of the features you have already built and killing underperforming features.

Nothing is ever really finished. It's just ready for its next iteration.

But It's Not Just About Iterating...

I'm kidding. It is just about iterating.

PART ONE:

VALIDATION

Products don't spring fully formed from your brain. Before your product, you have an idea. Sometimes it's a great idea. More often, it's a terrible idea.

The important thing is that you validate your idea—all of your ideas, really—before you jump in and start building your product.

The first section of this book is going to help you with that.

The meat of this section is going to deal with the most important thing you will ever do as an entrepreneur. It will teach you how to understand your customers.

This entire section is about validation. It includes techniques and tips for better customer development and user research, which will help you figure out what you're building and for whom you are building it.

Your lessons in validation are going to include how to figure out if your idea is any good, how to talk to a user, which users to talk to, and when to stop talking and start building.

In fact, you're going to learn all the things you need to do before you turn your idea into a product. Once you start doing them, you'll wonder why anybody ever builds a product any other way.

CHAPTER 1

Early Validation

In this chapter:

- Figure out if people will buy your product before you build it.
- Learn which research methods are best for early validation.
- Understand user pain in order to build a more compelling product.

Most startups begin with an idea for a fabulous new product. Most startups also fail. These two things may be more connected than you think. The problem is that the vast majority of startup ideas are based on things that somebody thought sounded cool or interesting, rather than something that solves a real problem for real people. This is why companies need to spend time validating their key hypotheses as early as possible.

What is a hypothesis and why do you need to validate (or invalidate) it? A hypothesis is an assumption that you're making. And, trust me, you are making a lot of assumptions when you start a company. For example, you are almost certainly assuming that there are people who will want to purchase the product that you're building.

The problem is that some of these assumptions are wrong. If the ones you got wrong are important enough, you're going to be out of business. Let's talk a little bit about how to avoid building your company on a lot of invalid assumptions, shall we?

First, instead of thinking that you have to come up with a brilliant product idea out of thin air, I'd like you to shift your thinking a bit. Think about every product as a solution to somebody's problem.

Let's look at some examples. Word processors solved the problem that it was tough to edit something once we'd typed it. GPS navigation solved the problem that we were likely to get lost when away from our homes. Even Angry Birds solved the problem of how to deliver more pleasure hormones to our brains while we were stuck waiting for a train.

One of the most common mistakes that people make when thinking of a product idea is solving a problem that simply doesn't exist or that isn't bad enough for people to bother fixing it.

Whenever you hear about a company "pivoting"—which is Lean for "changing your product into something entirely different"—it simply couldn't get enough traction with its original idea, and it had to switch to something more promising.

Some pivots may be necessary, but you want to minimize them as much as possible. To be fair, you probably can't avoid them completely without learning to tell the future. And that's OK. It's the nature of startups to change, sometimes quite drastically. But typically, you get only so many pivots before you run out of money, so it's in your best interest to validate your idea early, while it's still relatively easy to change. In fact, the earlier you start to validate your idea, the less likely it is that you'll have to pivot later.

Figure 1-1. Validate early and often

Let's look at how you can do that.

A Market, a Problem, and a Product Walk into a Bar

Before diving into some practical tips for how to do early validation, let's go over the difference between a market, a product, and a problem.

A market is the group of people you think might want to buy your product. For example, if you are building a tool to help tax professionals or real-estate agents or school teachers, that's your market.

Figure 1-2. A market

A problem is the reason that those people are going to use your product. If your product doesn't solve some sort of a problem for people, then there is very little chance that they're going to bother to give you money.

Figure 1-3. A problem

A product is simply the way that you're going to solve the user's problem. It's the end result of what you're building. It's the thing that people, presumably in the target market, are going to pay you money for.

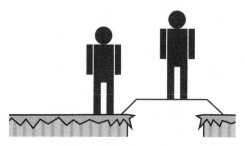

Figure 1-4. A product

I know this all sounds a little simple, but it's an important concept. A lot of startups are products in search of a market, and sometimes that works just fine. After all, how many people knew they needed to buy their books online before Amazon came along?

Other times, though, it can be disastrous. Every time a startup goes out of business because it "couldn't get traction" or it didn't "go viral," there is an excellent chance that there simply wasn't enough demand for the product because the product didn't solve a big enough problem for its market or it didn't solve the problem in a way that worked for users.

Because of this, it's important that you spend time validating the problem, the market, and the product as early as possible.

Validating the Problem

Let's imagine that, instead of spending time brainstorming brilliant ideas of products that nobody's ever thought of, you're going to go about finding a product idea in a totally different way. You are going to discover a problem that exists within your target market that you are capable of solving.

Remember, if there's no problem, then there is no compelling reason for people to purchase your product. Even if your idea is brilliant, innovative, and disruptive, early validation will help you refine your ideas and learn more about your users.

This isn't always easy to do. In fact, this may sound cryptic, but sometimes the best types of problems to solve are the ones that the users don't really know are problems until you fix them. How about an example to make that a little less confusing?

Before email came along, many of us did just fine communicating by phone or fax. It wasn't perfect, but we got things done that we needed to get done. Of course, if you tried to call someone in a foreign country or if you wanted to connect with lots of people at once, there were some pretty obvious drawbacks to the phone and fax model. But we lived with it, because it's what we had.

Then some genius came along and said, "What if you could type out the message you want to send and send it really far away or to dozens of people at one time?" That particular product solved a serious problem that most users couldn't have identified as a problem.

OK, sure. This probably isn't exactly how email was created. My point is that by using some of these techniques to observe potential users in interesting markets, you'll pretty quickly be able to identify some of the things that people are doing that you could make better. Once you've identified those things, it's much easier to come up with a product idea that people will like enough to use.

If you agree with Eric Ries—that "a startup is a human institution designed to deliver a new product or service under conditions of extreme uncertainty"—then think of early problem validation as something you do to reduce that uncertainty.

You can't guarantee yourself success, but early problem validation allows you to predict and avoid failure early in the process rather than after you've already spent all your investors' money.

You'll know that you've validated a problem when you start to hear particular groups of people complaining about something specific.

Validating the Market

Just because a problem exists doesn't mean enough people are going to be excited to pay for the solution. This is why you have to validate your market.

Your goal in validating your market is to begin to narrow down the group of people who will want their problems solved badly enough to buy your product. Your secondary goal is to understand exactly why they're interested so you can find other markets that might be similarly motivated.

Markets are notoriously difficult for startups to choose. There is a tendency among entrepreneurs to go for the broadest possible group of people who might be interested in purchasing a product. They will release a product aimed at "women" or "doctors" when what they should be doing is picking narrower markets like "urban moms who work full time outside the house and don't have nannies" or "oncologists in large practices who don't do their own billing."

By starting with smaller markets, you're more likely to find groups of people with very similar problems that will be easily solved by a small initial product. Don't worry if the initial market isn't very large. You can always expand your product later. Worry about finding a market with a single, overwhelming problem that you can solve.

You'll know that you've successfully validated your market when you can accurately predict that a particular type of person will have a specific problem and that the problem will be severe enough that that person is interested in purchasing a solution.

Validating the Product

Just because you have discovered a real problem and have a group of people willing to pay you to solve their problem, that doesn't necessarily mean that your product is the right solution. For example, millions of people want to lose weight, but that doesn't mean that every exercise and diet plan is guaranteed to be a big seller.

Validating your product tends to take much longer than validating your problem or market. This is an incredibly iterative process that I'll discuss in detail throughout the rest of the book.

The important thing is to keep coming back to the question, "Does this product really solve the identified problem for the specified market?"

You'll know that you've validated your product when a large percentage of your target market offers to pay you money to solve their problem.

Some Tools for Early Validation

Now that you know what you want to validate, let's look at a few useful tools for getting feedback about your problem, market, and product. Each of the following methods is a type of user research that is especially useful for this sort of early validation. In fact, they are all possible to perform long before you write the first line of code.

Ethnographic Studies (or, You Know, Listening to Your Users)

The most effective way to better understand the problems of your potential users is to go out and observe a few of them in person. You don't have to go all Jane Goodall and live amongst the chimps for years at a time, but you do have to spend some time getting to know the people for whom you are building a product.

This is your chance to ask open-ended questions about their problems and their lives. It's an opportunity to observe their behaviors and to learn what sorts of solutions they're currently using to solve their problem.

Here's an example. Many years ago, I did user research on a product aimed at people who process payroll for small businesses. Try not to nod off. It gets (slightly) more interesting.

While watching half a dozen people process the payroll for their businesses, several patterns emerged. The most important one, for the purposes of designing the product, was that *there was no pattern*.

Different users performed payroll tasks in completely different orders. Sometimes the same people would perform tasks in different orders during different payroll runs. It all depended on what needed doing that week. Sometimes they needed to add a new employee or terminate an old one. Sometimes they had all the information they needed, while other times they didn't. Often they'd get halfway through and have to go do one of a dozen different tasks. It was an incredibly nonlinear, interrupt-driven process.

This was not the kind of information we could have learned if we'd just asked people what was involved with processing payroll. This was the kind of information that we could get only by watching people go through it.

It turned out to be extremely useful information when designing the product, because it ended up having all sorts of implications for the way we saved user data and the way users accessed different parts of the product.

Learning about your users' problems is only a part of what you get when you do these sorts of ethnographic studies. You get a deep understanding of the people who make up your market, which you simply can't get from other forms of research.

Sure, you can observe how people do things, but you can also learn why they do them that way. One company that helps busy moms get deals on groceries spent quite a bit of time going shopping with women before it ever wrote a line of code. It learned about more than just coupon usage. It also learned the shopping patterns that women had—when they shopped, how many stores they went to, how often, and how they budgeted.

This sort of information allows you to build a product that not only solves a problem for users but that also fits naturally into their lives and schedules. It helps you build something that doesn't force users to learn new patterns in order to use your product, because your product fits seamlessly into their existing processes.

It can also help you invalidate ideas pretty quickly. For example, before we went to watch people process payroll, the product owners had come up with several ideas for making payroll more collaborative. However, once we started watching users perform their tasks, it became very clear that, for the types of businesses we were targeting, there was never more than one person performing the payroll tasks. Collaboration would have been a wasted feature unless the company decided to move into an entirely different market.

How you can do it right now

First, figure out who your target market is. Be specific. "Women" is not a good target market. There are simply too many of us, and we're all quite different from one another. Honest.

"People who process payroll for small businesses" is a great example of a market, since it's a clear job description. People who fit into that market are likely to have a lot of similar work-related needs. Another great example is "people who spend more than four hours a day on Facebook and play at least three different social games."

You will notice that these are large enough groups to be markets but are specific enough to have some very similar behavior patterns. That's important. Remember, this is a market to which you want to sell your product. If you want to sell a lot of your product, it makes sense to pick a market that has enough people to eventually support your growing business. The specific part is important because you want to be able to easily identify those people for your research.

A lot of people skip this very important step of identifying a potential market and just go out and talk to anybody they can find. This often includes friends, family, or random strangers on the street.

Here's why that's a terrible idea. Let's imagine you are interested in creating a product for people who drive cars. Now let's imagine that you find two people who will talk to you: One of them is a NASCAR driver, and the other is my mom. I guarantee that you will find virtually no overlap in what these two people are looking for in an automotive product. None.

On the other hand, if you find five NASCAR drivers or five grandmothers who live in the suburbs near their extended families, you are very likely to get quite a bit of overlap. That overlap is a pattern, and it's what allows you to make early decisions about what features your product should have and how you should market it to your potential users.

Now that you've picked your specific market, find five people who are in it. If you can't do this fairly easily, either you've picked too small a market, your market is too hard to reach, or you're just not trying hard enough. In any of these cases, rethink your career choices or find someone with some knowledge of the market to help you.

If one or two of the people you've identified are nearby, go visit them at their homes or offices or wherever you expect them to use your product. For those who don't live near you, do some sort of screensharing through something like Skype, GoToMeeting, or FaceTime, so that you can both talk to them and remotely view their surroundings.

Start off by asking them to show you how they currently perform some tasks that relate to the problem you're trying to solve. For example, you could ask them to walk you through exactly how they process their payroll. Meanwhile, you would ask them why they do things in a particular way and what other things they have tried.

Your goal is to get a good overview of their current practices and problems. It's also to spot patterns of behavior. Is there a specific problem encountered by each of the test participants? Have they all complained about a particular piece of software? Are they all performing tasks in a specific way that could be made easier?

Whatever observations you make and patterns you find, I guarantee this will change the way you think about your problem space and give you dozens of ideas for features that will make a truly useful product.

For example, one company I was working with wanted to create a new first-time user experience for its product. It felt that not enough people were making it through the registration funnel and becoming full members of the site. Before starting the project, the team members sat down and came up with dozens of ways they might close some of the holes in the funnel, but they weren't sure which way to go.

The thing is that they'd been through this process before with very little luck. They'd made lots of changes to the first-time user experience with very little to show for it in the way of improved metrics. So, instead of simply taking their best guess, as they had before, I recommended that they observe some users, both new and existing, and see if they could discover new ideas that might be likely to improve the user experience.

Unsurprisingly, after they'd observed five or six new users going through registration and spoken to a few current users, they discovered that the visual design of the registration process was giving new users an entirely different idea of what to expect than the actual product. New users going through the process assumed it was a product for children because of the fun, cartoon-like graphics. Serious, paying users of the product, on the other hand, tended to be older.

By changing the look and feel of the first few screens of the product, the team was able to significantly increase the number of qualified users who made it through registration and became full members of the site. It was as simple as not scaring away the types of people who would want to use their product, but it was not an insight that anybody on the team would have come up with without watching users.

The beauty of this method is that it takes very little work, and it can save you huge amounts of time later by making sure that you're solving a real problem that actually exists.

--- **NOTE** ---

The single greatest mistake you can make at this point is to start off by telling the test subject what you're working on and how great it will be for him. Nothing will bias a session faster than you trying to sell him on your ideas. *You're not there to talk. You are there to listen.*

Landing-Page Tests

OK, great. Now you've talked to some people, and you think you see a shared problem that you can solve. It's still not really conclusive evidence, right? I mean, what if those were the only five people in the world who have that problem? Or what if lots of people have the problem, but nobody's willing to pay you to help them solve it?

These are valid concerns, and you can address them long before you write the first line of code. The trick is to sell the product before you build it. Well, OK, technically that's kind of fraud, so how about you just advertise the product before you build it?

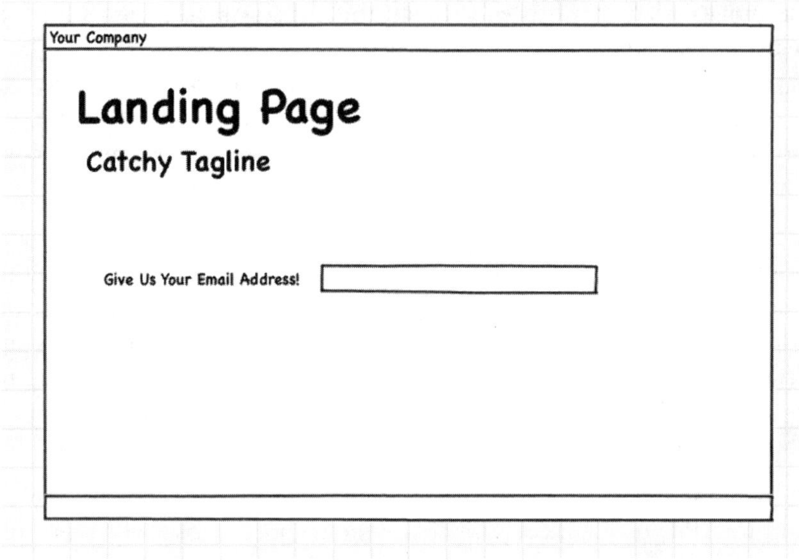

Figure 1-5. Do you have any idea how many of these you can make?

By building a few one-page sites, you can get a ballpark figure of the number of people who are interested in paying you to solve their problem. And the great thing is, you can start doing this before you start building anything. This means if nobody shows any interest in using your product, you can keep looking for new product approaches very cheaply until you find something that people are interested in using.

To be clear, I'm not just talking about direct-to-consumer Internet products here. Although you're using the Internet to advertise your ideas, you don't have to be building the next Amazon.

Have a concept for a premium day spa for pets? Why not build a website for it first and see how many people try to make reservations for Poodle Pedicures? It's a hell of a lot cheaper to build a landing page than it is to get salon chairs designed to fit a variety of dogs.

With landing-page tests, you can start to validate both your market and your product. By advertising a real thing (or several real things) that you are going to be selling, you're getting the best kind of feedback that people are willing to pay you for what you're making. You can also get a sense of which version of your product has the biggest potential market, which can be a huge advantage in deciding what to build first.

How you can do it right now

First, create a landing page that offers your magical (and fictional) product to the general public. Put a big button that says "Buy" or "Pre-order" on the landing page. For this, you may want to hire a decent graphic designer or artist who can make something that looks legitimate.

Alternatively, you can get decent designs from places like 99Designs or by using available free blog templates.

Drive a little traffic to your landing page with AdWords, Facebook ads, or any other method you think might get the right sort of people to view your offering.

Then check to see how many people click on your ads and what percentage of them click on your fake Buy button. Something like Google Analytics is useful and free to use for this purpose.

If you don't have any technical experience at all, you can do this with a Facebook page or use a service like LaunchRock, which will handle all the metrics stuff for you.

Prototype Tests

Great, by now you've validated that a particular group of people has a specific problem. You've also validated that they're willing to pay you to solve that problem, or at least are interested enough to sign up and give you their email addresses. You are way ahead of the majority of startups who are busy building something that nobody wants, but you still need to make sure the thing you're building solves the problem you validated.

I know that's a little confusing. After all, you've listened to people, you've tested their interest, and now you're building something that is specifically designed to solve their problems. Why on earth wouldn't it be right?

Because building products, even when you know what problem you're solving, is still hard. In fact, there might be hundreds of ways to solve the particular problem that you're addressing. You need to take the time to make sure that your approach and your implementation will actually end up working for your end users.

Here is the *worst possible way* for you to try to figure out if your idea solves somebody's problem: Ask them. The vast majority of entrepreneurs seem to think that explaining their concept in detail to a few people and then asking whether it's a good idea constitutes validation. It does not. People have a very hard time understanding a description of a product, and your friends may say your idea sounds pretty cool when you describe it to them. But it's an entirely different situation when potential users are confronted with a real product.

Here is the *best possible way* for you to try to figure out if your idea solves somebody's problem: Show them something and observe their reactions. Ideally, the thing you get in front of users will look and feel like the product, but you won't spend months writing code before you can start testing.

Let me back up. I've observed a large number of entrepreneurs doing what they think is product validation. This typically involves the entrepreneur excitedly describing exactly what his magical product is going to do. He often goes on and on until the potential customer's eyes have developed that sort of hunted look that you see when you corner an animal. At the end of the sales pitch, the entrepreneur "validates" the idea by asking, "So would that solve your problem?"

Even ignoring the fact that most of these potential customers would agree to practically anything just to get the entrepreneurs to shut the hell up, this is still the worst thing you can possibly do.

Nobody in the world can possibly tell you whether some abstract concept you just explained will solve a problem that they have. Even if they could somehow understand the wild abstractions you're presenting them with, they couldn't honestly tell you whether they would pay money for your solution. They just can't. You're asking them to predict what they will do in the future, and those of us who aren't psychic can't do that.

Don't believe me? Let's do an exercise. Let's say that I told you I was going to create the perfect way for you to lose 10 pounds, and it was going to be amazingly easy and cheap. Imagine what that looked like. I can now guarantee you that what you imagined is entirely different from what everybody else reading this book imagined. It's also almost certainly completely different from what I was talking about.

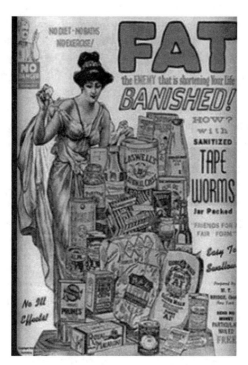

Figure 1-6. This isn't what you pictured, is it?

This is important because when you ask somebody to imagine something and then ask them if they would buy it, they answer by telling you whether they would buy their ideal imagined solution, not your actual product. Consider the above example. You might have bought something that fit your ideal product that would help you lose 10 pounds. You almost certainly wouldn't buy the real product.

So what's the alternative? Instead of describing what you're going to build, why not show them what you're going to build? Simply observing people interacting with a prototype, even a very rough one, can give you a tremendous amount of insight into whether they understand your potential product and feel it might solve a problem.

Prototype tests are the single best way to validate your product as early as possible. By validating early, you make sure that your product is compelling and usable while there's still time to fix it if it isn't.

How you can do it right now

I'll go more into various different methods of prototyping later in the book, but the important thing to understand here is that the closer you can get to showing people a real product, the more accurately you can predict whether people will use that product.

The most important thing is that whatever you're showing people has to be interactive enough that people can imagine they're using a real product. People have to be able to poke around the prototype by themselves and learn about what it might do for them without any interference from you. They have to be able to discover features and understand what the product is offering without you constantly chiming in and telling them what should be happening. The more you have to explain or describe what happens, the more you're going to bias the experiment.

Even at a reasonably high fidelity, though, an interactive prototype still takes far less time to build than an actual product. In later chapters, I'll give you some tips for how to balance speed and usefulness in developing the right sort of prototype for whatever you're testing. Won't that be fun?

Early Validation Isn't the End

So that's early validation, or at least a few examples of how to implement early validation. When Eric and Steve talk about getting out of the building, those are some very useful places to go and some reasonably easy things to do when you get there.

For those of you who think that's the end of the interaction that you need to have with your users, you are sadly mistaken. We're going to keep going back to those core ways of interacting with users throughout the development process. I'll even have some tips later in the book about how to get better at validation, so don't feel like this is the last you'll hear of these topics.

The important thing to remember is that you need to solve a real problem, and in order to find that problem, you need to listen to real people. It's nowhere near as easy as I'm making it sound, but the only way to get better at it is to do it. Over and over and over. Why not start now? I'll still be here when you get back.

Loosely Related Rant: Pain-Driven Design

I have a problem with both User-Centered Design and Customer-Driven Development (CDD). This may come as something of a shock to people, since I'm constantly giving advice on better ways to talk to users and to improve customer development efforts.

The problem I have with UCD and CDD is not the methods. The problem is that people so often misunderstand them. People hear "user centered" and think, for some insane reason, that we are encouraging them to turn their entire design process over to the user. They hear "listen to your customer" and think that we want them to blindly accept every ridiculous feature request made by somebody with a credit card and an opinion.

Guess what? I rarely speak for entire communities of people, but I think I can safely say that nobody in the User-Centered Design or Customer-Driven Development business is asking that of anybody. If they are, they're idiots and shouldn't be listened to anyway.

Unfortunately, a lot of us have debunked this myth by explaining that we don't really think that customers can predict future behavior (even their own) or that they're going to have some grand design vision for your product.

We just think that customers are great at talking about their problems and pain points, and that those are good things for you and your designers to know when you create a new feature or product.

I'm suggesting that we come up with a new name that will be harder (or at least more fun) to misinterpret: *Pain-Driven Design*.

What Is Pain-Driven Design?

The Pain-Driven Design (PDD) methodology requires that, before you start a design for a product or a feature, you need to figure out what is causing pain for your users and potential users. The desired outcome of PDD is to make that pain go away by some brilliant method of your devising. You then check to make sure you made your users' pain go away without causing them any more pain.

Is there a clever analogy?

There is! Imagine you're a doctor. You want to help people feel better. The first thing you need to do is talk to patients who come to see you.

Now, of course, you're not going to ask them what disease they have and how they think you should treat it. You're going to ask them, "Where does it hurt?" You're also probably going to ask them a lot of other questions about how they normally feel, what their medical history is, what their family is like, and other things like that. You'll probably also, if you're a good doctor, examine them, double-check their reported symptoms, and check for symptoms they may not even know they have.

Then, when you have figured out what is causing them pain, you will determine a good course of treatment that is likely to work based on your knowledge of various diseases, your extensive medical training, other work in the field, and how the patient reacts to treatments. You will then closely monitor their progress and adjust your approach as necessary.

Pain-Driven Design is a lot like that. You will talk to your users and potential users and find out what causes them pain when they are trying to solve a problem. You will interview them about their habits, likes, and dislikes. You will observe them using the product or competitors' products, looking for commonly appearing symptoms. You will then decide how to go about curing their pain. And, of course, you will closely monitor all your users to see how they respond to your treatment.

Since you have a large number of users, and there aren't any pesky rules against human experimentation in this context, you will run tests to see which treatment performs best.

Does it work before I have a product?

Sure it does! Presumably your eventual product will solve somebody's problem, yes? Maybe her problem is that it is too hard to find a great restaurant while traveling, or that she is sort of bored while waiting for the train. OK, those don't seem like big problems, but they are problems nonetheless and should have solutions.

Since you don't have a product yet, you need to figure out how people are currently solving this problem. Are they using a similar product? A completely different one? Are they simply suffering in silence without even knowing that their lives would be infinitely better if this problem would go away?

You can discover these things by asking people how they're dealing with their problems and what the pain points are with their current solutions (or nonsolutions). You can learn more about their pain by watching them suffer through it. Don't worry, it's not so bad to watch them suffer, because you know your product will help them!

What if I already have a product?

It still works! You see, no matter how much you love your product, unless it is perfect it's causing pain to somebody. I'm sure it's not on purpose. You're not a monster. But something about your product is confusing or hard to use, and it's driving at least one of your customers crazy.

Again, examine them. Find out when they feel the most pain while using your product. Watch brand new people use your product to see how much pain it takes to learn. Watch old customers use your product to figure out what weird workarounds they've created to avoid the pain you're causing them.

Find all the pain points. Then come up with devastatingly clever ways to fix them.

What if my product is disruptive?

Often people think this doesn't apply to them because their product is so wildly different from anything else on the planet that it's solving a problem users don't even know they have. Or it's revolutionizing something or other that will transform how humans interact with everything.

But the product is still solving a problem, right? Even if it's solving that problem in a completely novel way or solving it for a new group of users, presumably if people are going to adopt the product, the product will be solving a particular problem for them.

That's great. Even if people have never seen anything like your product, you can get a huge amount of information by talking to users about how they currently solve their problems as well as their general environment for problem solving. And once your disruptive product has been launched, chances are it's causing some people pain, so you should observe people interacting with it to learn where the pain points are.

What if my customers try to tell me how to fix their problems?

Well, I suppose you could plug your ears and scream loudly so that you won't be in danger of hearing them talk about their solutions. Or you could listen to their solutions and then politely follow up to make sure you understand the underlying pain that they're trying to cure.

Frankly, I prefer the latter approach, but it's up to you.

One interesting thing that I've found in my many, many years of listening to customers is that sometimes the customers are right about the solution. I know; crazy! I mean, we've been assured by hundreds of people that listening to customers' solutions is completely useless and that they're always wrong!

Guess what? They're not.

This doesn't mean you should take their word as gospel, but I can't imagine that people within your company have a patent on coming up with the right solutions to customer problems. Just because an idea for a solution comes from a user doesn't automatically make it useless or wrong, even if the anti-UCD crowd seems to think so.

How will Pain-Driven Design be misinterpreted?

Who can say? I sort of hope somebody reads only the title of this rant and writes a scathing retort about how I'm a horrible person for advocating that designers be subjected to pain until they come up with better designs (note: They shouldn't, except in certain very specific cases, and they know who they are).

Or maybe they'll dissect my doctor/patient analogy and point out all the ways in which it's flawed (note: There are 17 ways...see if you can spot them all!) and thereby conclude that, since my analogy isn't perfect, my methodology must also be crap.

But I hope a few people will say, "Hey, that Pain-Driven Design methodology is just a catchy name for understanding our customers' problems so that we can come up with better solutions!" And more importantly, I hope a lot of people will say, "You know, that Pain-Driven Design sounds like a great idea, and we should try it in our organization!"

Go Do This Now!

- Learn from your users before you build: Try a contextual inquiry or a customer development interview.

- Test your market early: Try a landing-page test.

- Figure out what sort of pain you're causing customers: Try some observational usability on your product or a prototype.

CHAPTER 2

The Right Sort of Research at the Right Time

In this chapter:

- Learn which research is right for your product at every phase of its lifecycle.

- Get tips about some unusual research methods that will save you time and money.

- Understand what you're almost certainly doing wrong when you're talking to users.

I get a lot of startups and entrepreneurs who come to me wanting to "do more user research." While it's great that they want to do the research, it's unfortunate that they don't have any idea about what kind of research they should be doing. While the last chapter covered the sorts of research you should do for early validation of an idea, let's talk about some other research techniques.

There are hundreds of different ways to collect information about your users. Some of them would be useful for you to do right now. Some would be a giant waste of money. Do you know the difference?

```
Landing Pages                    Product Stubs (Fake Doors)
Guerilla User Tests                    Task Based Usability
    Wizard of Oz                    Brain Imaging (yes, really!)
                    Analytics
New User Interviews                          A/B Testing
            Customer Development Interviews
Prototype Usability                    Observational Usability
    NPS Surveys          Sales          Click Tests
Unmoderated Testing      Focus Groups        Surveys
```

Figure 2-1. Here are a few types of research. Think you know which is right for you?

Of course, this is a problem that is experienced only by product owners who actually want to do research in the first place. I just as frequently hear people say something along the lines of, "Oh, we don't have time to do user research."

Well, guess what, genius? If you don't have time to do user research, you'd better make time to fix your product once you've built it wrong, because I guarantee that is what's going to happen. The fact is, you don't have time *not* to do research.

I'll give you an example, but I want you to realize that this is only one telling of the same story I've heard a thousand times.

A company I spoke with had just released a completely new user interface for its expensive enterprise product. Because it was an expensive enterprise product, it had a limited number of very serious, committed users who had paid tens of thousands of dollars to use the product.

The company felt that its product had a very dated look, and it was time for a visual refresh. As with so many things that are "just a visual refresh," this update changed several fairly major things about the product, including how users accessed their files.

When the management showed me the new look, I asked them how much usability testing they had done before releasing the new feature. "None," they said. "We had a really tight deadline, and we didn't have time."

Next, I asked what the user reaction had been. "Not good."

Unsurprisingly, changing the way users accessed files without first understanding how users were accessing their files caused a few problems. The biggest problem was that users immediately started complaining and demanding a change back to the old version. Presumably, this was not the reaction the company was hoping for with its big, expensive redesign.

What ended up happening may seem familiar. The company spent several weeks doing damage control and figuring out a way to redesign the redesign in order to get back the functionality that users missed. It also spent a lot of time soothing customers, who were paying them lots of money, and reassuring them that this would not happen again.

Of course, if the company continues not running usability tests on its designs, it can pretty much count on it happening again. And again, and again.

The really sad part of this story—and all the others like it—is that maybe a week of user research could have prevented most of the problems. The company presumably could have avoided changing key user functionality by observing customers using the product. It could have found out immediately that it was breaking an important user paradigm simply by having a few users click through some mockups of the design.

In other words, it could have saved a huge amount of time and money by getting it right the first time!

And that is the simple truth—if you're doing the right sort of research at the right time, you will end up saving time and money.

So now we've decided that research is incredibly important and that it can be very difficult to figure out which type is right for your product at this exact point in time. Let's take a look at some great options for getting feedback on your product.

I already touched on a couple of different types of user research you should be doing: customer validation and prototype testing. Now I'd like to share a few incredibly fast methods for testing your ideas that you may not have considered.

Competitor Testing

Who are your competitors? Don't give me any of that, "We don't have any competitors! We're disruptive!" nonsense. I get it. You're a unique snowflake. Now knock it off and figure out who your competitors are.

If you really can't think of anybody else who's close to you, think of some products that might be used by the same type of person you're targeting.

Now go test them.

Even Your Competitors Make Mistakes

That's right. I said test somebody else's product. You're not going to fix it for them. You're going to avoid all the mistakes they're already making.

You see, regardless of how great they are or how much market share they have, your competitors are screwing something up. This is your chance to exploit their weaknesses.

Not only does this help point out mistakes you shouldn't make as well, but it can also provide a way to really nail down your core product. For example, this is an extremely useful technique to use in enterprise software or any sort of complex application. If you can isolate the 10% of a complicated product that people use all the time, you can deliver an infinitely simpler product with an elegant user interface that will destroy the big, bloated monstrosities that people have grown to hate.

The really beautiful thing about this sort of testing is that you can do all sorts of it before you have a product. Hell, you can do it before you have an idea for a product. This is a fantastic way to learn about some serious user problems that you are totally capable of fixing.

How You Can Do It Right Now

This one is easy. Run some Google, Facebook, or Craigslist ads to find four or five people who are already regular users of your competitors. If they're nearby, go visit them. If they're remote, get on some sort of video chat with screensharing. Schedule it at a time when they'd naturally be using your competitor's product.

Then just watch. After you've watched for a while, ask them some questions. Here are some good ones to ask, but feel free to come up with your own based on what you just watched:

- What do you like about that product?
- What do you hate about it?
- What confuses you about it?
- What do you find particularly annoying about it?
- What's missing from it?
- How did you learn to use it?
- Where did you hear about it?
- Have you tried anything else like it?
- Why did you pick this particular product over the other options?

- (For enterprise products) What parts of your job do you still have to do outside the product? How do you feel about that?

Five-Second Tests

Another super fast, cheap, and easy test you can do is testing what users think you do. Remember, you already know what your product does. But you'd be shocked by how many of your users have literally no idea who you are, what your product is, or why they should be using it. The horrifying thing is, they often feel this way after they've seen your actual product.

One of the most critical decisions that you're going to make as a startup is how you talk to users about your product. How do you explain what it does? How do you get them to understand the benefits and features you're providing? This is your messaging, and you need to be testing it from the very beginning. That starts with your landing page.

The reason landing pages are so important is that they are your first, and sometimes only, chance to turn a visitor into a user. If someone hits your landing page and bounces, that's lost potential revenue.

Whether you're trying to persuade people to sign up for a web-based service or to order a product online or to call a sales rep for a demo, chances are that you are losing potential users on your landing page, not because people don't want what you're selling, but because they don't know what it is.

The goal of your landing pages should be to convert the right sort of visitors into users. Metrics can tell you whether you're doing a decent job of this. A/B testing can tell you which of your various landing pages are doing best.

But none of that will tell you *why* your landing pages are converting the way they are. The only way to find out why users are reacting to your landing pages the way they are is to answer the following questions:

- What does the user think this product does?
- Who does the user think the product is for?
- Can the user figure out how to get the product?

In other words, you need to test your messaging, your branding, and your call-to-action (CTA).

You might wonder why you need to test things like messaging and branding. After all, you probably paid a nice visual designer to come up with something awesome. You may have hired a copywriter to craft some wonderful verbiage. You probably sat around a conference room and discussed these things at length.

But the problem is, your visual designer and your copywriter and your entire team know what your product does. That person who is visiting your landing page for the very first time and is maybe giving you a few seconds of her precious time? Not so much.

You need to figure out if that painfully crafted prose and that gorgeous visual design actually convey anything to a drive-by visitor. And to do that, you need to get some screens in front of real people in a way that lets you judge their very first, unbiased reactions.

How You Can Do It Right Now

There are a couple of really simple ways to do this. The first involves ambushing strangers.

Go to your local coffee shop, deli, bar, or other place you can approach people without looking too creepy or getting arrested. Bring your computer or tablet with a few versions of your landing pages. Dress appropriately. Bring cash.

Ask people if they will look at a couple of screens for your startup in exchange for a beverage. Assure them you're not selling anything. Show them your landing pages.

Then ask them variations on the questions I listed before, such as the following:

- What does this product do?

- Who is this product for?

- What would you do if you came to this page on the recommendation of a friend or after clicking on an ad?

Feel free to follow up with polite questions about what makes them think those things. Don't be mean about it. Do remember to buy them a beverage.

If you'd like to solicit more opinions than you can get in your neighborhood, there's a product by a company called UsabilityHub that I've used effectively to do this same sort of thing. It's called FiveSecondTest.

Just post a static mockup of your landing page, type in those three questions, and request 10 or 15 test subjects. Then go away for a little while.

While you're waiting, users who come to the Usability Hub site will be shown your landing page for exactly five seconds. They will then be asked the questions you specified. You'll get a nice summary of how they answered each question and a tag cloud of the most commonly used words.

It's quite simple and incredibly cheap. And the lovely part is, you'll find out exactly what impression you're giving users in that critical first few seconds when they're deciding whether to bother signing up to use your product or not.

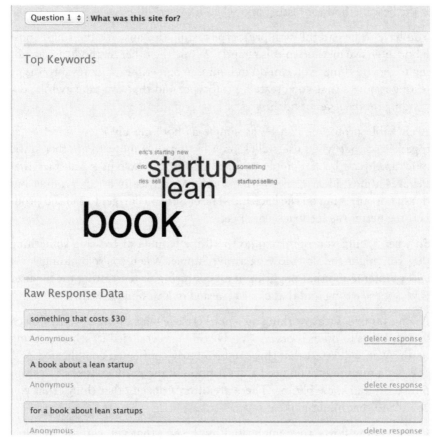

Figure 2-2. Guess what book we were testing here?

Clickable Prototype Testing

Have you ever been using a product and trying to perform some task and just gotten completely lost and frustrated? If you answered no, I want you to think about the fact that you just blatantly lied in response to a hypothetical question posed by a book. Who does that?

Now, I want you to realize that the vast majority of really frustrating tasks can be completely avoided before a product is ever shipped. The way you do this is by prototyping out the most common tasks and testing them before you ever write a single line of code.

I touched on prototype testing in the previous chapter when we discussed early validation, but right now I want to talk about when prototype testing is the best method for testing and when it's overkill.

You have to be careful with prototype testing, because it's the single most labor-intensive method in this chapter. While the other methods you're going to see are things you can do in hours, or sometimes minutes, prototype testing requires that you create a prototype, and that can take awhile, depending on the level of fidelity.

A clickable prototype can be as simple as hooking up a few wireframes together so that when users click on a button they move to another static mockup. It can be as complicated as building a whole user interface that behaves almost identically to what a user would see in a real product but doesn't do anything on the backend. The closer you can get to the end product, the better the feedback you'll get.

So when would you bother to go to all the trouble of creating something that you might end up throwing away? Simple: When you're building some sort of interaction that might be at all confusing or frustrating for the user if you got it wrong and that can't be tested in any simpler way.

As an example, I was working on a marketplace where people were allowed to sell things to other users. Anybody who has ever tried to sell something on the Web will attest that this can be a fairly confusing, complicated process. At a minimum, you need a description of the product, a price, a shipping cost, and some photos. There are often a dozen other things that you could add that might make it sell faster.

Often, selling flows are complicated by the fact that you can sell multiple different types of things, each of which might require different information. Selling a toaster requires different information from selling a car.

Because of all this interaction, there are potentially dozens of different places where a user could get confused. The only real way to test to see if you've covered all your bases is to watch some users go through the process on their own.

Waiting until the product is fully baked to do this means that if you got something wrong (note: You got something wrong), changing it will take extra engineering work. If you got it really wrong (note: There's a good chance you got it really wrong), you could end up throwing everything out and redoing the whole thing.

Personally, I'd rather throw out my quickly built prototype than weeks of engineering work. I've found that engineers also prefer this. Kind of a lot.

On the other hand, there are times when you wouldn't bother making a fully interactive prototype. For example, a landing page often involves nothing more than some messaging and a simple call-to-action that allows someone to log in or sign up for your product.

It's not that you don't want to test this. You absolutely must, and I've already given you a couple of nice, easy ways to do it. It's that it can often take the engineers as little time to build the real page as it would take you to build a fake one. If it's extremely easy to change (in other words, if you're working in a system with continuous deployment, rollback, and good metrics, which you totally should be because you're Lean, right?), sometimes just shipping the damn thing and testing on real users makes the most sense.

And, yes, I acknowledge that there are acres of gray area between these two examples. At some point you're going to have to use your judgment. Here are some useful guidelines for times you'd absolutely want to create an interactive prototype:

- For some reason it will be difficult or slow to change it in production if you got it wrong—for example, you're shipping software in a box or building a physical product.

- Your finished product could kill someone or otherwise have a terrible outcome if it's wrong—for example, you're building a medical device or an election ballot.

- The expected user flow is more complicated than a single click or call-to-action—for example, the user has to move through several states or input various pieces of information, each of which may affect later decisions.

- You have engineers who will be upset if they have to throw away all their work because you designed it wrong—for example, every engineer I have ever met.

How You Can Do It Right Now

Step 1: Make an interactive prototype. There are a lot of ways to do this. I'm not going into all of them because other people have already done it. I like HTML and JavaScript for high-fidelity prototypes. Other people like Axure. One person once liked Flash, I think, although I never met him.

The trick is to pick something that you can build in quickly and iterate on. Remember, you probably are going to get something wrong and need to change it. You'll want something that lets you do that fast.

A few people build prototypes in things like PowerPoint or Keynote. These people are wrong. Prototypes built using tools that are meant for something entirely different are notoriously hard to maintain, and designers who do this often spend twice as much time fighting with their platform as they do actually designing good experiences. Using a tool that is meant for creating truly interactive experiences is going to be much, much faster in the end, even if you have to spend some time up front learning to use it.

Step 2: Decide who to interview and what tasks to perform. I'm not going to go into this process in detail, since there are a thousand books, like *Observing the User Experience* by Mike Kuniavsky (Morgan Kaufmann), that can teach you about recruiting and moderation and creating perfect tasks.

The most important thing here is to figure out what tasks you want to test and then ask some strangers to try to perform those tasks with your product. Feel free to use current users of your product, if you have any. They are going to be fantastic at telling you whether your new model fits in with their current behaviors.

A few of the things that I find myself testing on any product that has them include the following:

- Signup flows that have more than one step
- Purchase flows
- Searching and browsing experiences—for example, finding a particular product
- Sharing experiences—for example, taking a picture or leaving a comment
- File uploads and editing
- Navigation of the entire product
- Physical buttons on products that aren't entirely screen based
- Installation for products that require any kind of setup
- Anything else that requires more than one or two steps

Step 3: Have three to five people whom you've recruited perform several tasks that you've decided to test. You can do this in your offices, in their homes or offices, or remotely using screensharing software like GoToMeeting.

For example, if you're testing a checkout flow, you'd ask each participant to use your prototype to try to purchase an item. Then you would watch them attempt to perform that task, take notes about where they got confused, and ask them to tell you how they felt about the process.

Once you've identified a few major problems that users are having while completing the tasks, fix the prototype, and do it all again. Keep iterating until users are able to complete most tasks without crying.

If you have a few versions of the prototype with various user experiences, you can even ask test participants to perform the same tasks on each prototype to see which one performs best. Don't forget to show the prototypes in different orders to different participants. Everybody will perform the task better on the third prototype than the first one, because they will have learned something about the product.

Guerilla User Tests

Once upon a time, user testing was expensive and time consuming. You would rent a lab with a big one-way mirror and an expensive video system. You would hire an expert like me to ask your users questions and assign them tasks. The expert would write up a 30-page report and maybe a PowerPoint deck with dozens of things that you should change about your product. And then...well, nothing, generally. Nobody would ever read that report, the deck would be lost on a server somewhere, and everything would go back to the way it was.

Frankly, it was just incredibly depressing.

That's why one of my favorite innovations is the guerilla user test. Guerilla user testing is cheaper, faster, and far more actionable. It is fantastic for very quickly finding major usability flaws in the key parts of your product.

In other words, you can see all the ways that new users are struggling to understand what they're supposed to be doing.

Because of the nature of guerilla testing, you're unlikely to test on current users, so make sure that you're using it to test new user problems like onboarding, messaging, or early conversion.

Of course, it's going to be significantly more effective for products that don't require a lot of specialized knowledge. I don't know that I'd bother testing that new missile launch system at the local Starbucks, unless that Starbucks happens to be right next door to NASA.

How You Can Do It Right Now

Load your interactive prototype, actual product, or somebody else's product onto your laptop, iPad, or mobile phone and go to your favorite coffee shop. Offer to buy somebody a coffee if they'll spend 10 minutes looking at your product.

Once you have a victim, give her a single task to perform. Give her only the amount of data she'd be likely to have if she came to the task herself. For example, if you're asking somebody to test your photo-sharing app, make sure she's used Facebook or Twitter before and she understands what it means to share a photo.

Then let her perform the task while you watch. Don't help. Don't prompt. Don't give her a demo. Don't spend five minutes explaining what your product does. Just let her try to perform the task. Observe where she gets stuck. Listen to the questions she asks (but don't answer them yet!). Ask her how she thinks the task went when she's done.

Then buy her a coffee, thank her, and find another person.

By the time you've run four or five people through the task, you should have an excellent sense for whether it has any major usability flaws and what they are. If everybody breezes right through the task, well done! Get yourself a coffee. Maybe a muffin, if they look fresh. Then pick another task you're curious about and run five more people through it.

If, on the other hand, you started to see a pattern of problems from the five people you ran through the task, go back to your office and figure out a way to solve the problem. Fix the prototype or product. Then test it again to see if you improved things.

One word of caution: You can't actually learn whether people will *like* your product this way. You can only figure out if people understand your product. But, frankly, that's a pretty important thing to know.

Loosely Related Rant: Shut the Hell Up and Other Tips for Getting Feedback

I have spent a lot of time telling you to ask people questions and get feedback. Unfortunately, this is another one of those things that seems like it would be incredibly easy to do, but everybody gets it wrong.

For example, I was talking to an engineer who was describing his startup's first experience in trying to get user feedback about its new product. Since it was a small company and the product didn't exist in production yet, the company had these goals for gathering user feedback:

- Get information about whether people thought the product was a good idea.

- Identify potential customer types, both for marketing and for further research purposes.

- Talk to as many potential users as possible to get a broad range of feedback.

- Keep it as cheap as possible!

He had, unsurprisingly, a number of stories about mistakes they had made and lessons they'd learned during the process of talking to dozens of people. As he was sharing the stories with me, the thought that kept going through my head was, "*Of course* that didn't work! Why didn't you [fill in the blank]?"

Obviously, the reason he had to learn all this from scratch was because he hadn't moderated and viewed hundreds of usability sessions or had any training in appropriate user-interview techniques. Many of the things that user researchers take for granted were brand new to him.

In order to help others who don't have a user-experience background not make those same mistakes, I've compiled a list of five things you're almost certainly doing wrong if you're trying to get customer feedback without much experience.

Even if you've been talking to users for years, you might still be doing these things, since I've seen these mistakes made by people who really should know better. Of course, this list is not exhaustive. You could be making dozens of other mistakes, for all I know! But just fixing these few small problems will dramatically increase the quality of your user feedback, regardless of the type of research you're doing.

Shut the Hell Up

This is the single most important lesson to learn when interviewing people about anything. You are interviewing them. You are not talking. You are listening. You want their opinions, not your own. To get those, you have to shut the hell up and let them give you their opinions without becoming hostile or defensive or explanatory.

You also need to give them more time than you think to figure things out on their own, and that's easier to do without somebody babbling in their ear.

Remember, while you may have been staring at this design for weeks or months, this may be the first time your participant has even heard of your product. When you first share a screen or present a task, you may want to immediately start quizzing the participant about it. Resist that impulse for a few minutes! Give people a chance to get their bearings and start to notice things on their own. There will be plenty of time to have a conversation with the person after he's become a little more comfortable with the product, and you'll get more in-depth comments if you don't put him on the spot immediately.

Don't Give a Guided Tour

One of the most common problems I've seen in customer interviews is inexperienced moderators wanting to give way too much information about the product up front.

Whether they're trying to show off the product or trying to "help" the user not get lost, they start the test by launching into a long description of what the product is, who it's for, what problems it's trying to solve, and all the cool features it has. At the end of the tour, they wrap up with a question like, "So do you think you would use this product to solve this exact problem that I told you about?" Is there any other possible answer than, "Ummm...sure?"

Instead of the guided tour, start by letting the user explore a bit on his own. Then give the user as little background information as possible to complete a task. For example, to test a new shopping app, I might give the user a scenario they can relate to, like: "You are shopping online for a new pair of pants to wear to work, and somebody tells you about this new app that might help. You've just loaded it onto your phone from the App Store. Show me what you'd do to find that pair of pants."

The only information I've given the user is stuff he probably would have figured out if he'd found the product on his own and installed it himself. I leave it up to the users to figure out what the app is, how it works, and whether or not it solves a problem that they have.

Ask Open-Ended Questions

When you start to ask questions, never give the participant a chance to simply answer yes or no. The idea here is to ask questions that start a discussion.

These questions are bad for starting a discussion:

- "Do you think this is cool?"
- "Was that easy to use?"

These questions are much better:

- "What do you think of this?"
- "How'd that go?"

The more broad and open ended you keep your questions, the less likely you are to lead the user and the more likely you are to get interesting answers to questions you didn't even think to ask.

Follow Up

This conversation happens at least a dozen times in every test:

Me: "What did you think about that?"

User: "It was cool."

Me: "WHAT WAS COOL ABOUT IT?"

User: [Something that's actually interesting and helpful.]

Study participants will often respond to questions with words that describe their feelings about the product but that don't get at why they might feel that way. Words like "cool," "intuitive," "fun," and "confusing" are nice, but it's more helpful to know what it was about the product that elicited that user reaction. Don't assume you know what makes a product cool!

Let the User Fail

This can be painful, I know. Especially if it's your design or product that's failing. I've had engineers observing study sessions grab the mouse and show the participant exactly what to do at the first sign of hesitation.

But the problem is, you're not testing to see if somebody can be *shown* how to use the product. You're testing to see if a person can *figure out* how to use the product. Frequently, I've found I learned the most from failures. When four out of four participants all fail to perform a task in exactly the same way, maybe that means the product needs to change so they can perform the task in the way that is apparently most natural.

Also, just because a participant fails to perform a task immediately doesn't mean that she won't discover the right answer with a little exploration. Watching where she explores first can be incredibly helpful in understanding a participant's mental model of the application. So let her fail for a while, and then give her a small hint to help her toward her goal. If she still doesn't get it, you can keep giving stronger hints until she's completed the task, or you can just move on to the next thing while making a note that you've found something you need to fix.

Are those all the tricks to a successful user study? Well, no. But they're solutions to mistakes that get made over and over, especially by people without much experience or training in talking to users, and they'll help you get much better information than you would otherwise.

Go Do This Now!

- Learn from your competitors' mistakes: Try conducting a usability test on somebody else's product.

- Get feedback on your idea or product today: Try one type of user research on whatever you're working on right now.

- Get better at talking to users: Try having someone sit in on your user interviews and give you feedback about what you're doing wrong.

CHAPTER 3

Faster User Research

In this chapter:

- Learn how to get research results faster without sacrificing quality.
- Find out when it's safe to use remote or unmoderated testing.
- Understand the right way to run surveys.
- Feel superior to people who refuse to do research for several awful reasons.

Now you know some ways to do the right kinds of user research at the right time for your company. That will save you a huge amount of time right there, because you won't be wasting time doing the wrong type of research.

But can we make it even faster? I think we can.

Regardless of the type of user research you're doing—from observational studies to five-second landing-page tests—you can make your research far more efficient with some simple rules.

Iterate! Iterate! Iterate!

I used to run a lot of usability tests for clients. One time I was asked to participate in a particular test. "OK," I said, "so we'll be recruiting six to eight test participants, right? That way, if we get a couple of no-shows, we'll still have plenty of people to get good data."

That's when they surprised me. The client wanted a "statistically significant" test. They wanted to talk to at least 35 people.

Now, let me be perfectly clear. I was a contractor. I was getting paid by the hour, and this client wanted me to sit through 35 hours of testing, rather than the five or six I would have recommended.

I begged not to do it. It was, I explained, an enormous waste of the client's money. We did it anyway. It was an enormous waste of the client's money.

Honestly, this is a composite story of many times when clients have asked me to do many, many sessions of testing in a row. Inevitably, what happens is the following:

- We do a few tests.

- A few really obvious problems crop up.

- In every subsequent session, we learn the exact same things about the obvious problems and have a very hard time getting any other information because the big problems are sucking all the focus away from any smaller problems we might have found.

Imagine if you are testing your product. You have 10 people scheduled to come in, one right after the other. You realize in your first test that nobody can log in to your product because of a major UX failure. How useful are those other nine tests going to be? What could you possibly learn from them—that all 10 people can't log into your product? Couldn't you have learned that from the first person?

Here's the key: Patterns start to emerge in usability research after the first few tests. After five, you're really just hearing all the same stuff over and over again.

But here's another important tip: Once you remove those major problems that you find in your first few tests, you can start to find all the other problems with your product that were blocked by the original big problems.

So, for maximum efficiency in any type of user research, you want to find the minimum number of people you can interview before you start to see a pattern. Then you want to interview that many people over and over, leaving plenty of time between sets to make changes to your product, mockup, prototype, discussion guide, or whatever else you're testing.

There is one more important note! There are a couple of types of research where you might want to have larger numbers of participants in each round of iteration (although, you never want as many as 35...just never). For example, things like five-second tests can take 10 or 15 people before you start to see patterns. This is fine, since they're incredibly cheap and fast to run.

How You Can Do It Right Now

When you set up your next research plan, whether it's usability testing of a prototype or customer validation on a particular type of user, recruit a small number of participants in a fairly short amount of time—no more than a couple of days.

Run those sessions, and then stop and analyze your information. Look for patterns or problems. If you're doing usability testing, try making some changes to your prototypes to fix the obvious usability flaws you have discovered. If you're doing five-second testing, change your messaging or images to address any confusion you're causing users. If you're doing customer validation, think of some new types of questions you want answered based on the input you've received so far.

Then do it again.

In strict usability testing, you're going to keep repeating this pattern until your test participants can get through all the tasks with relative ease and minimal confusion. For customer validation, you keep doing this until you think you've identified a serious problem for a specific market that you think you can solve. In landing-page tests, you keep going until people look at your landing page and actually understand what your product does.

Whatever type of research you're doing, keeping it small and then iterating will always give you the best return in the least amount of time.

Stay in the Building

Getting out of the building doesn't always require actually getting out of the building. In fact, sometimes staying in the building can be far more efficient. No, I haven't suddenly lost my mind. This makes sense.

While visiting users' homes or offices can yield wonderful information, many times remote research can give you what you need in far less time, and at a far lower cost. You just need to determine whether the type of research you're doing really requires being in the same room with the subject.

For example, many types of prototype usability testing can be done remotely with screensharing tools like GoToMeeting, Skype, or Join.me (or a dozen others). Often customer development interviews can be done over the phone.

The only types of research that absolutely have to be done in person are the ones where you need to understand the environment in which a user will be accessing your product or when a test subject needs to be in the same room as the product—for example, many mobile applications or products that are meant to be used onsite, like in a doctor's office or a factory.

Besides the cost and time savings, remote research has the added benefit of allowing you to get feedback from users all over the world. This is a huge advantage if you have global users.

How You Can Do It Right Now

Instead of scheduling a test participant to come to your office or making an appointment to go to her, send her a link to a screensharing session and give her a call.

Just make sure when you're testing a prototype that it's accessible to the other user, either through the screenshare or on a server somewhere. You need to have a setup that allows the test participant to manipulate the prototype. This isn't a demo; it's a test.

If you have a mobile app that can be downloaded, you can ask the subject to turn on her webcam so that you can watch her use the product. It's not perfect, by any means, but it will allow you to test with people who aren't in your immediate vicinity.

Of course, anytime you use extra technology, you should make sure you've run through the process once or twice before trying it with a real test participant. If you're using something like GoToMeeting or WebEx, make sure you've started a session before and learned all the controls, so you don't spend the first half of the test troubleshooting your testing tools.

Unmoderated Testing

The last few years have seen the creation of a whole host of new products designed to help you get feedback without ever having to interact with a user. Used correctly, unmoderated testing tools can help you get certain types of fantastic feedback very quickly and cheaply. Used incorrectly, they can waste your time and money.

Unmoderated testing is a way to automatically get a video of a real human using your product and attempting to perform various tasks that you assign. These are obviously aimed at web-based products, although at least one company has made it possible to test mobile apps this way, as well.

You just need to provide a link to your product, a few tasks for the user to perform, and a credit card. After a few hours, you will receive video screen captures of real people trying to perform those tasks while narrating what they're trying to do.

Because there is no recruiting, scheduling, or moderating on your part, you can get usability feedback within hours rather than days.

Before you run out and start using unmoderated tests, let's review what they are fantastic for:

1. Finding out if your product is easy enough to use that a person who has never seen your product before can come in and immediately perform an assigned task.

Now let's review what they are terrible for:

1. Finding out if people will like your product.

2. Finding out if people will use your product.

3. Finding out if people, when left to their own devices and not given any instructions, can figure out what task they're supposed to perform while using your product.

4. Finding out how real users of your product are using your product on a daily basis.

5. Finding out how to fix the usability problems you uncover.

6. Everything else.

Here's an example of a time when I used UserTesting.com, one of the many testing services, to uncover and correct a serious design problem.

I was designing a flow to allow a user to sell something online. It's the kind of thing that doesn't seem like it would be tough to get right until you actually try selling something online and realize how horrible most marketplace sites are.

I designed the flow and tested it in prototypes, so I was fairly confident that it would go well. As soon as it was live on the site, we ordered up three UserTesting.com users and asked them to go to the site and try to list something for sale.

Interestingly, the flow for selling something went really well, just like in the prototype tests. The problem that we saw immediately, though, was that users were taking far too long to find where to start the selling flow in the first place.

Luckily, they were consistent about failing to find the feature. They all went to the same (wrong) place. Of course, what this meant was that they weren't the ones who were wrong. We were!

We quickly made a change to allow users to start the selling process in the more obvious (to the users) place, ran three more users through unmoderated tests, and came up with a clean bill of health on the feature.

Of all the things that we did on that product, the one piece of feedback we consistently got was how incredibly easy it was to list things for sale. That almost certainly wouldn't have been the case if users had never been able to find the feature in the first place.

How You Can Do It Right Now

First, pick the right sort of thing to test. Ideally, you want a few simple tasks that a new user might perform on a product that is available on the Web.

Your goal for this test is to understand whether somebody new to your product can quickly figure out how to accomplish a task. Remember, this is straight usability testing. It's not going to tell you anything about whether anybody is going to like or use your product.

Also, if your product requires a specific type of user, this may not be ideal for you. You can use one of the companies, like UserTesting.com or OpenHallway, that allows you to recruit your own users, but doing that removes one of the benefits of this type of testing, which is that it doesn't require you to do any recruiting.

Once you've got the right sort of tasks, find one of the dozens of blog posts that compare the different unmoderated usability testing options out there. I've used UserTesting.com, but there are lots of options, like Loop11 and TryMyUI, and they all have pros and cons. If you want to do this type of testing on mobile, there are fewer options, but keep checking. More companies are being started every day, but books don't get updated often enough for me to give you a complete list.

Now go through the hopefully well-tested process for starting a test.

You'll most likely be notified that the test is complete within an hour or two. The site should provide you with some sort of video that you can watch. So, you know, watch it. Even better, watch some of the videos with your whole team so that they can all experience firsthand exactly the problems that your users are having.

Then fix those problems and do it all over again until you can stop cringing at the pain your users are feeling.

When to Survey

Frequently when I ask entrepreneurs if they're in touch with their users, they say something along the lines of: "Oh, very in touch. We do surveys all the time." Then I count to 10 and try not to imagine murdering them.

Surveys do not count as being "in touch with your users." They don't. Let me explain why. In the vast majority of surveys, *you* are the one setting the answers. In other words, if you ask somebody "What's your favorite color? Red, blue, or yellow?" you're going to miss out on everybody whose favorite color is orange. You're not even going to know that orange exists as an option.

"Aha!" the surveyors say, "We can combat that by just giving people an 'other' option!" Sure, except that you're wildly underestimating how badly you're biasing people's answers by first presenting them with some standard answers. This is especially true if you're asking something like "What do you hate about the site?" If you present them with a bunch of things they're likely to hate, most people will simply choose a preselected answer.

"Fine," the surveyors go on, irrationally undaunted, "but what if we just allow them to type in their answer in a text box instead of giving them preset answers?" You know what people hate doing? Writing. Look, if I see a long survey with nothing but a bunch of open text boxes, I will simply leave, and I am the kind of person who writes a book! Stop expecting your users to do all your work for you by typing lots of long answers into a survey. There are things they'll be thrilled to tell you on the phone that they would never type into a web form.

Let's be perfectly clear. As with so many other tools, surveys can be extremely useful, but they're not a replacement for listening to customers talk about their needs or watching people use your product.

They are, however, a great way to quickly follow up on patterns you spot in the qualitative research you should be doing.

Here's an example. A colleague and I were doing some preliminary research on the attitudes and behaviors of female angel investors. We wanted to learn more about their motivations and see if those motivations differed at all from those of male angel investors. To that end, we interviewed several female angels, male angels, and some wealthy women who could conceivably have made an angel investment but hadn't.

But, of course, we didn't interview all female angels. We didn't even interview a statistically significant number of them. You see, this sort of qualitative research isn't a statistically significant science experiment. It often doesn't have to be. All it has to do is present you with some likely hypotheses you can later test in a more thorough manner.

As with the vast majority of this sort of research, we started seeing very early patterns. After speaking with around five people in each group, we had some interesting hypotheses. Based on this, we decided to run a survey to see if the patterns held true over a larger group or if we had somehow found a very biased group of test participants to interview.

We ran a survey asking a few simple follow-up questions about things like gender and whether they had ever been asked to make an angel investment. We asked some specific, factual questions that the participant could answer easily and a few slightly more complicated questions that asked people about their attitudes toward angel investing.

Most importantly, the goal of the survey was not to generate new hypotheses about why women did or did not make angel investments. The goal was to validate or invalidate the hypotheses that we had formed during our initial research.

Surveys are great at reaching a large number of people very quickly, so they are fantastic for following up on ideas and patterns that you spot initially in qualitative research. However, because of the structure of the questions and answers, they are often terrible for helping you to spot patterns or form hypotheses about important topics like how users feel or what new features users would like to see.

How You Can Do It Right Now

First you need to figure out what question you want answered. Is it something like, "What is the most confusing part of my product?" Do you want to know which feature to build next? Do you want to learn more about what other products your customers use on a daily basis?

Once you've determined your question, recruit around five of the right sort of person to answer that question. If it's a question about power users, recruit power users. If it's a question about your product's first-time user experience, recruit people who are in your persona group but who have never seen your product before.

Then do your research. There are lots of books on how to run basic user ethnography or usability testing. This is not one of them, but the basic gist is to interview them about the questions you have. Watch them use the product. Talk to them about their likes and dislikes. Basically, ask a lot of open-ended questions and do a lot of observing.

Once you've noticed patterns or come up with some very specific questions that you want answered by a larger group of people, you turn those questions into a survey.

Don't forget to include some screening questions to make sure you're getting answers from the right sorts of people. For example, if you only care about how women feel about something, you should probably ask for the participant's gender as one of your questions.

By using qualitative research to generate your hypotheses and realizing that surveys are only good at validating or invalidating those hypotheses, you can turn surveys into an incredibly powerful tool. Just don't try to use them to come up with new ideas. They're the wrong tool for that.

Loosely Related Rant: Stupid Reasons for Not Doing Research

Almost every company I talk to wants to test its products, get customer feedback, and iterate based on real user metrics, but all too often they have some excuse for why they just never get around to it. Despite people's best intentions, products constantly get released with little to no customer feedback until it's too late.

Whether you're doing formal usability testing, contextual inquiries, surveys, A/B testing, or just calling up users to chat, you should be staying in contact with customers and potential customers throughout the entire design and development process.

To help get you to stop avoiding it, I've explored six of the most common stupid excuses for not testing your designs and getting feedback early.

Excuse 1: It's a Design Standard

You can't test every little change you make, right? Can't you sometimes just rely on good design practices and standards? Maybe you moved a button or changed some text. But the problem is, sometimes design standards can get in the way of accomplishing your business goals.

For example, I read a fascinating blog post by a developer who had A/B tested the text on a link. One option read, "I'm now on Twitter." The second read, "Follow me on Twitter." The third read, "Click here to follow me on Twitter."

Now, anybody familiar with "good design practices" will tell you that you should never, ever use the words "click here" to get somebody to click here. It's *so* Web 1.0. But guess which link converted best in the A/B test? That's right. "Click here" generated significantly more Twitter followers than the other two. If that was the business goal, the bad design principle won hands down.

Does this mean that you have to do a full-scale usability and A/B test every time you change link text? Of course not. Does it mean you have to use the dreaded words "click here" in all your links? Nope. What it does mean is that you should have some way to keep an eye on the metrics you care about for your site, and you should be testing how your design changes affect customer behavior, even when your changes adhere to all the best practices of good design. So to put it simply: Prioritize what you care about and then make sure you test your top priorities.

Excuse 2: Company X Does It This Way

I can't tell you how many times I've heard, "Oh, we know that will work. Google/Facebook/Apple does it that way." This is the worst kind of cargo cult mentality.

While it's true that Google, Facebook, and Apple are all very successful companies, you aren't solving exactly the same problem that those companies are, you don't have exactly the same customers that they do, and you don't know if they have tested their designs or even care about design in that particular area.

You are, hopefully, building an entirely different product, even if it may have some of the same features or a similar set of users.

Is it OK to get design ideas from successful companies? Of course it is. But you still need to make sure *your* solutions work for *your* customers.

I previously worked with a company that had a social networking product. Before I joined them, the company decided that, since other companies had had good luck with showing friend updates, they would implement a similar feature, alerting users when their friends updated their profiles or bought products.

Unfortunately, the company's users weren't very interested in the updates feature as it was implemented. When we finally asked them why they weren't using the feature, the users told us that they would have been very interested in receiving an entirely different type of update. This was later backed up by metrics when we released the new kind of update. Of course, if the company had connected with users earlier in the process, it would have rolled the feature out with the right information and gotten a much more positive reaction on launch.

Another thing to remember is that just because a company is successful and has a particular feature doesn't mean it's that exact feature that makes it successful. Google has admitted that the "I'm Feeling Lucky" button loses it page views, but it keeps it because the company, and its customers, like the feature.

That doesn't mean it's a good business plan for your budding search engine startup to adopt a strategy of providing people with the equivalent of the "I'm Feeling Lucky" button. In fact, this is a great example of why you might need to employ multiple testing methods: qualitative testing (usability, contextual inquiry, surveys) to find out if users find the feature compelling, and quantitative testing (A/B, analytics) to make sure the feature doesn't bankrupt you.

The bottom line is it doesn't matter if something works for another company. If it's a core interaction that might affect your business or customer behavior, you need to test it with your customers to make sure the design works for you.

Obviously, you also need to make sure that you're not violating anybody's IP, but that's another book.

Excuse 3: We Don't Have Time or Money

As I have pointed out before, you don't have time *not* to test. As your development cycle gets farther along, major changes get more and more expensive to implement.

If you're in an Agile development environment, you can make updates based on user feedback quickly after a release, but in a more traditional environment, it can be a long time before you can correct a major mistake, and that spells slippage, higher costs, and angry development teams.

I know you have a deadline. I know it's probably slipped already. It's still a bad excuse for not getting customer feedback during the development process. You're just costing yourself time later.

Excuse 4: We're New; We'll Fix It Later

I hear this a lot from startups, especially Agile ones, that are rushing to get something shipped, and it's related to the previous excuse. Believe me, I do understand the pressures of startups. I know that if you don't ship *something* you could be out of business in a few months. Besides, look at how terrible some really popular sites looked when they first started! You have to cut something, right?

Great. Cut something else. Cut features or visual polish. Trust me, people will forgive ugly faster than they'll forgive unusable. Whatever you decide to cut, don't cut getting customer feedback during your development process. If you ship something that customers can't use, you can go out of business almost as fast as if you hadn't shipped anything at all.

Potential users have a lot of options for products these days. If they don't understand very quickly all the wonderful things your product can do for them, they're going to move on. Take a few hours to show your ideas to users informally, and you will save your future self many hours of rework.

Excuse 5: It's My Vision; Users Will Just Screw It Up

The fact is, understanding what your users like and don't like about your product doesn't mean giving up on your vision. You don't have to make every single change suggested by your users. You don't have to sacrifice a coherent design to the whims of a vocal individual.

What you should do is connect with your users or potential users in various different ways—user tests, contextual inquiry, metrics gathering, etc.—to understand whether your product is solving the problem you think it is for the people you think are your customers. And, if it's not, it's a good idea to try to understand why that is and develop some ideas for how to fix it.

Besides, how many people do you think spent months creating their perfect vision, then shipped it and realized that nobody else was seeing the same thing they were?

Excuse 6: It's Just a Prototype to Get Funding

This is an interesting one, since I think it's a fundamental misunderstanding of the entire concept of customer research. When you're building a prototype or proof of concept, you still need to talk to your customers. The thing is, you may have an entirely different set of customers than you thought you did.

Maybe you think the target market for your new networked WiFi lunchbox is 11- to 13-year-old girls, but they're not going to pay you to build the first million units and get them into stores. Your first customers are the venture capitalists or the decision makers at your company or whoever is going to look at your product and decide whether or not to give you money.

Even if they're not your eventual target market, it's probably a good idea to spend some time talking with whomever you're trying to get to fork over the cash. I'm not saying you should change your entire product concept based on this feedback. I mean, if you really want to start the company on your credit cards and a loan from your mom, don't change a thing! The important takeaway here is that you may have different audiences at different points in your company's life. And the best way to find out what they all want is to talk to them!

Out of Excuses?

Those are the most common excuses I hear, but I'm sure you can think of some clever ones. Then again, your time is probably better spent connecting with your users, understanding their problems, and thinking of ways to address them.

Go Do This Now!

- Learn from a distance: Try running a remote or unmoderated test and compare your results with in-person research.

- Run a (good) survey: Try creating a survey based on hypotheses generated by qualitative research.

- Confront your own reasons for not doing research: Try to think of all the excuses you have for not talking to customers this week. Now do the research anyway.

Qualitative Research Is Great...
Except When It's Terrible

In this chapter:

- Learn when to do qualitative research and when to do quantitative.

- Understand the best approach for figuring out what features to build next.

- Learn what type of research will help you predict whether users will buy your product.

I have now spent several chapters telling you that you will burn in hell if you don't do qualitative research on your users. I'm now going to tell you when that advice is absolute poison. Aren't you glad you didn't stop reading after the first few chapters?

The truth is that qualitative research isn't right for every situation. It's fantastic for learning very specific types of things, and it is completely useless for other things. That's OK. The trick is to use it only in the right circumstances.

First, let's very briefly touch on some of the differences between qualitative and quantitative research. Qualitative research is what we've been mainly discussing so far in this book. It typically involves interviewing or watching humans and understanding their behavior. It's not statistically significant.

Here are a few examples of qualitative research:

1. Contextual inquiry

2. Usability studies

3. Customer development interviews

Quantitative research is about measuring what real people are actually doing with your product. It doesn't involve speaking with specific humans. It's about the data in aggregate. It should always be statistically significant.

Here are a few examples of quantitative research:

1. Funnel analytics

2. A/B testing

3. Cohort analysis

I know we haven't gone into what any of those quantitative research methods are or how you might accomplish them. If you're interested in learning more about these sorts of analytical tools (and you should be), you may want to check out the book *Lean Analytics* by Alistair Croll and Ben Yoskovitz (O'Reilly).

But none of that matters unless you understand when you would choose to use a qualitative method and when you would choose to use a quantitative method. Quantitative research tells you *what* your problem is. Qualitative research tells you *why* you have that problem.

Now, let's look at what that means to you when you're making product decisions.

A One-Variable Change

When you're trying to decide between qualitative and quantitative testing for any given change or feature, you need to figure out how many variables you're changing.

Here's a simple example: You have a product page with a buy button on it. You want to see if the buy button performs better if it's higher on the page without changing anything else. Which do you do? Qualitative or quantitative?

Figure 4-1. How could you possibly choose?

That's right, I said this one was simple. There's absolutely no reason to qualitatively test this before shipping it. Just get this in front of users and measure their rate of clicking on the button.

The fact is, with a change this small, users in a testing session or a discussion aren't going to be able to give you any decent information. Honestly, they probably won't even notice the difference. Qualitative feedback here is not going to be worth the time and money it takes to set up interviews, talk to users, and analyze the data.

More importantly, since you are changing only one variable, if user behavior changes, you already have a really good idea *why* it changed. It changed because the CTA button was in a better place. There's nothing mysterious going on here.

There's an exception! In a few cases, you are going to ship a change that seems incredibly simple, and you are going to see an enormous and surprising change in your metrics (either positive or negative). If this happens, it's worth running some observational tests with something like UserTesting.com, where you just watch people using the feature both before and after the change to see if anything weird is happening. For example, you may have introduced a bug, or you may have made it so that the button is no longer visible to certain users.

A Multivariable or Flow Change

Another typical design change involves adding an entirely new feature, which may affect many different variables.

Here's an example: You want to add a feature that allows people to connect with other users of your product. You'll need to add several new pieces to your interface in order to allow users to do things like find people they know, find other interesting people they don't know, manage their new connections, and get some value from the connections they've made.

Figure 4-2. Do you know these people?

Now, you could simply build the feature, ship it, and test to see how it did, much the way you made your single-variable change. The problem is that you'll have no idea *why* it succeeded or failed—especially if it failed.

Let's assume you ship it and find that it hurts retention. You can assume that it was a bad feature choice, but often I find that people don't use new features not because they hate the concept, but because the features are badly implemented.

The best way to deal with this is to prevent it from happening in the first place. When you're making large, multivariable changes or really rearranging a process flow for something that already exists on your site, you'll want to perform qualitative testing before you ever ship the product.

Specifically, the goal here is to do some standard usability testing with interactive prototypes, so that you can learn which bits are confusing (note: Yes, there are confusing bits, trust me!) and fix them before they ever get in front of users.

Sure, you'll still do an A/B test once you've shipped it, but give that new feature the best possible chance to succeed by first making sure you're not building something impossible to use.

Deciding What to Build Next

Look, whatever you take from this next part, please do not assume that I'm telling you that you should ask your users exactly what they want and then build that. Nobody thinks that's the right way to build products, and I'm tired of arguing about it with people who don't get UCD or Lean UX.

However, you can learn a huge amount from both quantitative and qualitative research when you're deciding what to build next.

Here's an example: You have a flourishing social commerce product with lots of users doing lots of things, but you also have 15 million ideas for what you should build next. You need to narrow that down a bit.

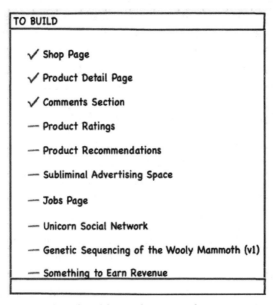

Figure 4-3. This shouldn't take more than 20 or 30 years

The key here is that you want to look at what your users are currently doing with your product and what they aren't doing with it, and you should do that with both qualitative and quantitative data.

Qualitative Approaches

- Watch users with your product on a regular basis. See where they struggle, where they seem disappointed, or where they complain that they can't do what they want. Those will all give you ideas for iterating on current features or adding new ones.

- Talk to people who have stopped using your product. Find out what they thought they'd be getting when they started using it and why they stopped.

- Watch new customers with your product and ask them what they expected from the first 15 minutes using the product. If this doesn't match what your product actually delivers, then either fix the product or fix the first-time user experience so that you're fulfilling users' expectations.

Quantitative Approaches

- Look at the features that are currently getting the most use by the highest-value customers. Try to figure out if there's a pattern there and then test other features that fit that pattern.

- Try a "fake" test by adding a button or navigation element that represents the feature you're thinking of adding, and then measure how many people click on it. Instead of implementing an entire system for making friends on your site, add a button that allows people to Add a Friend, and then let them know that the feature isn't quite ready yet while you tally up the percentage of people who are pressing the button.

Still Don't Know Which Approach to Take?

What if your change falls between the cracks here? For example, maybe you're not making a single-variable change, but it's not a huge change either. Or maybe you're making a pretty straightforward visual-design or messaging change that will touch a lot of places in the product but that doesn't affect the user process too much.

As many rules as we try to make, there will still be judgment calls. The best strategy is to make sure that you're always keeping track of your metrics and observing people using your product. That way, even if you don't do exactly the right kind of research at exactly the right time, you'll be much more likely to catch any problems before they hurt your business.

Loosely Related Rant: If You Build It, Will They Buy It?

As you have hopefully figured out, I'm a huge proponent of qualitative user testing. I think it's wonderful for learning about your users and product.

But it's not a panacea. The fact is, there are many questions that qualitative testing either doesn't answer well or for which qualitative testing isn't the most efficient solution.

Unfortunately, one of the most important questions people want answered isn't particularly well suited to qualitative testing.

If I Build It, Will They Buy?

I get asked a lot whether users will buy a product if the team adds a specific feature. Sadly, I always have to answer, "I have no idea."

The problem is, people are terrible at predicting their future behavior. Imagine if somebody were to ask you if you were going to buy a car this year. Now, for some of you, that answer is almost certainly yes, and for others it's almost certainly no. But for most of us, the answer is, "It depends on the circumstances."

For some, the addition of a new feature—say, an electric motor—might be the deciding factor, but for many the decision to buy a car depends on a lot of factors, most of which aren't controlled by the car manufacturer: the economy, whether a current car breaks down, whether we win the lottery or land that job at Goldman Sachs, etc. There are other factors that are under the control of the car company but aren't related to the proposed feature: Maybe the new electric car is not the right size or isn't in our price range or isn't our style.

This is true for smaller purchases, too. Can you absolutely answer whether or not you will eat a cookie this week? Unless you never eat cookies (I'm told these people exist), it's probably not something you give a lot of thought to. If somebody were to ask you in a user study, your answer would be no better than a guess and would possibly even be biased by the simple act of having the question asked.

Admit it, a cookie sounds kind of good right now, doesn't it?

There are other reasons why qualitative testing isn't great at predicting future behavior, but I'm not going to bore you with them. The fact is, it's simply not the most efficient or effective method for answering the question, "If I build it, will they come?"

What Questions Can Qualitative Research Answer Well?

Qualitative research is phenomenal for telling you whether your users can do X. It tells you whether the feature makes sense to them and whether they can complete a given task successfully.

To a smaller extent, it can even tell you whether they are likely to enjoy performing the task, and it can certainly tell you if they hate it. (Trust me, run a few user tests on a feature they hate. You'll know.)

This obviously has some effect on whether the user will do X, since he's a lot more likely to do it if it isn't annoying or difficult. But it's really better at predicting the negative case (i.e., the user most likely won't use this feature in its present iteration) than the positive one.

Sometimes qualitative research can also give you marginally useful feedback if your users are extremely likely or unlikely to make a purchase. For example, if you were to show them an interactive prototype with the new feature built into it, you might be able to make a decent judgment based on their immediate reactions if all of your participants were exceptionally excited or incredibly negative about a particular feature.

Unfortunately, in my experience, this is the exception rather than the rule. It's rare that a participant in a study sees a new feature and shrieks with delight or recoils in horror. Although, to be fair, I've seen both.

What's the Best Way to Answer This Question?

Luckily, this is a question that can be pretty effectively answered using quantitative data, even before you build a whole new feature. A lot of companies have had quite a bit of success with adding a "fake" feature or doing a landing-page test.

For example, one client who wanted to know the expected purchase conversion rate before it did all the work to integrate purchasing methods and accept credit cards simply added a buy button to each of its product pages. When a customer clicked the button, he was told the feature was not quite ready, and the click was registered so that the company could tell how many people were showing a willingness to buy.

By measuring the number of people who thought they were making a commitment to purchase, the client was able to estimate more effectively the number of people who would actually purchase if given the option.

The upshot is that the only really effective way to tell if users will do something is to set up a test and watch what they actually do, and that requires a more quantitative testing approach.

Are There Other Questions You Can't Answer Qualitatively?

Yep. Tons of them.

The most important thing to remember when you're trying to decide whether to go with qualitative or quantitative is to ask yourself whether you want to know what is happening or why that particular thing is happening.

If you want to measure something that exists, like traffic or revenue or how many people click on a particular button, then you want quantitative data. If you want to know why you lose people out of your purchase funnel or why people all leave once they hit a specific page, or why people seem not to click that button, then you need qualitative.

Go Do This Now!

- Go from quant to qual: Try looking at your funnel metrics to understand where you are having problems, and then run a qualitative study to understand why users are having problems in those places.

- Go from qual to quant: Try making a change based on your qualitative research learnings and measuring that change with an A/B test.

DESIGN

Hey, did you know that the word "design" is right there in the subtitle of this book? It's true. I guess that means it's probably time to stop talking about research and start talking about what you do with all that knowledge you've been collecting and how you might start turning those ideas into something more solid.

I appreciate your patience.

In case you skipped Part One, we're going to assume that you have done your research. You know who your customer is. You know what her problem is. You think you know how to solve that problem.

Part Two of this book is going to deal with design. It's going to take you on a whirlwind tour through all the parts of design you're going to need in order to get a product built.

This section covers everything from the nuts and bolts of building a prototype to figuring out when you don't want one. It talks about what sort of design you shouldn't be doing, since that can save you an incredible amount of time and hassle. It even covers a bit of visual design.

And yes. I couldn't get away with having Lean in the title if I didn't talk about Minimum Viable Products. Those get their own chapter.

Don't get me wrong. You're not anywhere near done with the validation process. But now that you've got a fully validated idea, isn't it time to start building and validating your product? I think it is.

CHAPTER 5

Designing for Validation

In this chapter:

- Learn why you should design a test before you design a product.

- Get nine tools that are critical for designing your product.

- Understand which of those tools you can safely skip depending on what you're building and for whom.

I should warn you, if you're already a professional designer of any sort, you may find some of the following tedious or infuriating. That's OK. This isn't meant to teach professional designers to be even better at their jobs. This is meant to teach other people how to do enough design to validate or invalidate their initial hypotheses. It's also meant to teach designers how to design in Lean environments and validate their work.

Design is a rich and complicated field that people study for their whole lives with varying degrees of success. Even worse, there are dozens of different disciplines within design—for example, figuring out how a complicated product should work is different from designing a beautiful brochure, which is different from designing a physical object. These are all called design. Probably because we are designers and not linguists.

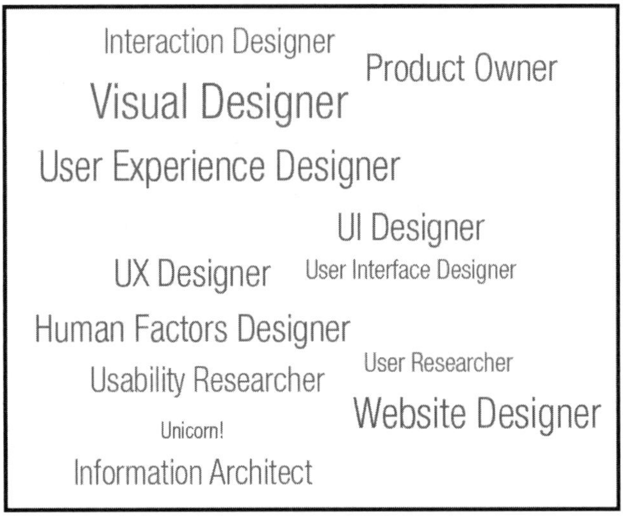

Figure 5-1. Why designers shouldn't be allowed to name things

But, at its heart, design is about solving problems. Once you've defined your problem well and determined what you want your outcome to be, Lean UX encourages you to do as little work as possible to get to your desired outcome, just in case your desired outcome isn't exactly perfect. That means doing only the amount of design you need to validate your hypothesis.

Sometimes doing very little design is even harder than doing a lot of design. Because the trick is knowing what sort of design is the most important right this second and what is just a waste of time.

If you've done your research, you should understand your problem, your market, and your product concept pretty thoroughly. You hopefully have a problem you want to solve and an idea of a feature or product that might solve it. Now you need to build something.

Maybe this should be obvious, but there are all sorts of different kinds of things that you need to build over the course of a product's life span. A lot of advice just focuses on the very first time you build something—the initial product.

But the vast majority of design decisions happen after you've built a product. You are constantly iterating and changing your initial product. Or, at least, you should be.

Here are some of the things you will have to do in the course of building and rebuilding your product. All of these require some amount of design:

- Fix a bug.

- Deal with an error state.

- Make a small change in a user flow.

- Create an entirely new feature.

- Do a complete visual redesign.

- Tweak an existing visual design.

- Reorganize the product.

- Build a whole new product.

- Redesign for another platform.

Just to make things even more confusing, there is a whole lot of gray area between some of these. For example, some bug fixes are typos, others fundamentally change the process a user goes through, and some may not have any obvious user impact at all.

But all these different types of changes have one very important thing in common: In Lean UX, you should be designing just enough to validate your hypothesis. And no more.

There is a process for doing this in a Lean way, and I'm going to describe it here. As I describe it, you're going to be thinking to yourself, "This seems like a huge amount of work!"

And the thing is, it *is* a lot of work. Lean design is not lazy design. It's not about skipping steps or doing a shoddy job or not thinking through the user experience. In fact, Lean UX has a huge amount in common with traditional User-Centered Design and also with Agile Design, neither of which are particularly easy.

I started this section by writing a step-by-step guide for designing a product, but I kept wanting to write, "The next step is X except for when it isn't." That's when I realized that this sort of design is not a linear process. It's a set of tools.

Sometimes, in the course of building a product or a feature, you'll use all these tools. Sometimes you'll skip one or two steps. That's OK. The key is to understand the tools well enough to know when it's safe to skip one.

Tool 1: Truly Understand the Problem

The first tool in any sort of design is truly understanding the problem you want to solve. In this way, Lean UX is no different from any other sort of design theory. Sadly, it's pretty different from the way a lot of people practice design.

The vast majority of time I talk to entrepreneurs, they present me with solutions rather than problems. They say things like, "I want to add comments to my product," not "My users don't have any way to communicate with one another, and that's affecting their engagement with my product."

By rephrasing the problem from your user's point of view, you help yourself understand exactly what you are trying to do before you figure out how to do it.

I'm not going to rehash how you might understand the problem you're trying to solve. If you're confused by this, go back and read Chapters 2 through 5. I'll give you a hint: It involves listening, observation, and other sorts of research.

One note to make here is that often research won't be confined to just users. We've been talking a lot about listening to your users, and that is clearly the most important thing you can be doing. But this is the point where you also need to listen to stakeholders within your company.

If you're part of a small startup, luckily this will be quick. Make sure that you have involved the people in your organization most likely to understand the problem you're trying to solve. These people could be practically anybody in the organization—customer service folks, engineers, and salespeople are obvious choices if they exist.

Just remember that there are people within your organization who may understand the problem better than you do, and make sure that you're incorporating their knowledge into the design process. They're not creating the final designs or telling you exactly what people need. They're weighing in with their thoughts about business needs, and their input should be weighed against the input from the customers.

Let's imagine that you already have a product with some people who are using it. However, as with many startups, you are getting signals that your product is confusing. For example, many people visit your product or download your app and then never use it again. That's a good sign that you're not solving the problem people thought you'd be solving for them. Your first step is to start by understanding the problem better.

For example, you need to figure out your user base:

- What sort of people are using your product?
- How familiar with technology are they?
- Are you mainly trying to help new users or existing users?
- Are they paying you or using your product for free?

You need to understand the context in which they'll be using your product:

- Are they looking for quick help on the go or are they at a desk and ready to commit time to learning about your product?
- Do they need help from an expert, or will help from other users work?
- Are they likely to have problems in the middle of something critical and time sensitive?

You need to learn more about your user needs:

- Are they using your product for fun? For work? To make themselves more productive?

You may already know the answer to a lot of these questions, but don't assume the same is true of any problem you're trying to solve for your users. Figure out the types of users, context, and needs for any specific problem you're trying to solve. You'll use all of this information in all of the following steps.

When Is It Safe to Skip This?

It is never, ever safe to skip this. If you don't understand the problem, you can't solve it.

Tool 2: Design the Test First

If I had to pick one thing that really sets Lean UX design apart from all other sorts of design, it would be this. Lean UX always has a measurable goal, and you should always figure out how to measure that goal before you start designing. If you don't, how will you know that your design worked? Here's a real-life example. Once upon a time, I worked at IMVU. For those of you who don't know, IMVU allows its users to create 3D avatars and chat with other people from around the world. Users customize their avatars with all sorts of virtual goods, like clothes, pets, and virtual environments.

As with all companies, we occasionally had to decide what to work on next. We decided that our first priority was to increase a specific metric—activation. We wanted more folks who tried the product once to come back again.

So our goal for the project was to increase the activation number.

We needed to figure out how we would know if the project was a success. We decided that our project would be a success when we saw a statistically significant increase in the percentage of new users coming back within a certain amount of time.

To fully understand whether the problem was fixed by our new design, we'd release any changes we made in an A/B test that would show the old version to half the new users and the new version to the other half. We'd measure the percentage of folks coming back from both cohorts over a period of several weeks and see what happened.

Now we knew our problem, and we had a verifiable way to know that we'd either solved the problem or made progress toward solving the problem.

I'm not going to go into all the different ways that we tried to make progress on that specific metric. I'll have more on those sorts of changes later. Suffice it to say that some things moved the needle and others didn't. More importantly, it wasn't always the biggest changes that had the biggest impact. The point was, whatever changes we made, we had an objective way of determining whether or not the design was a success.

There are other sorts of tests you might do rather than a strict A/B test, and I'll cover those later in the book.

Interestingly, desired outcomes aren't always obvious and A/B tests aren't always possible. In our example of helping people who are having problems, looking at the number of problems people are solving isn't really a good metric. I mean, you could easily increase the number of problems people are solving by increasing the number of problems they're having, and that is not a metric you want any higher.

A better metric in this case might be something like the number of support calls you get from users who see the new feature or the number of questions you get about specific problems users were having.

The trick is that all success metrics must be measurable and directly related to your business goals. Again, I'll talk more about how to pick a good test goal later in the book. Think of it as an annoying little trick to force you to keep reading.

When Is It Safe to Skip This?

You really shouldn't skip this either, although I've found that this particular exercise can take as little as a few minutes. Before you start to design or build anything, you should know very clearly what it is intended to do and how to know whether it is working.

Tool 3: Write Some Stories

A lot of times when we think of stories, we think of the very specific Agile engineering stories that we write and track. These are not the sort of stories you're going to write.

You need to write down design stories. Think of these as a way to break down your problem into manageable steps. Also, think of these as a way to evaluate the design once it's finished.

A good story for our user help experiment might be something like, "Users who are having trouble making changes to their accounts can quickly figure out how to solve that problem."

Don't forget to write admin stories, too! You might include something like, "Customer service reps can more quickly add new content to help users when new problems arise."

You'll notice I didn't suggest things like, "Customers can ask questions of other users and get immediate responses." That may be a solution that you explore, but being too explicit about how you're going to solve your problem can lock you into a specific idea too soon and prevent you from discovering better ones.

When Is It Safe to Skip This?

Writing down stories is always a good idea. With that said, you're welcome to skip writing stories for very trivial things like quick bug fixes; small changes to messaging; or visual design changes, like testing a new button color, that are better represented by showing the actual design.

On the other hand, the very simplest stories should take no more than a few minutes to write, so consider doing it anyway, just as practice. Sometimes, in the process of writing design stories, you'll find that you're missing a crucial part of the design.

For example, I was talking with a startup that was changing its home page rather dramatically. The team thought it was a very simple visual design change. However, once they started writing their stories, they realized that one part of the design involved testing different images on the home page. They also realized that they wanted to allow their marketing team to continue to test different images going forward, which meant that they needed an admin interface to allow that to happen. By writing the design stories, they thought through things like how changes would be made going forward—things they would otherwise have missed.

Tool 4: Talk About Possible Solutions with the Team

Depending on the type of person you are, this is either the most fun or the most tortuous part of the design process. I'm not going to go into detail about the best way to discuss things with your team, but make sure that it's a very small, targeted group of people who have a strong grasp of the problem you're trying to solve.

If you've properly used Tool 1 in this chapter, you're already ahead of the game. You've talked to these stakeholders already when you were in the process of truly understanding the problem.

The important thing here is that, just because you know the exact problem you're trying to solve, doesn't mean there's a single, obvious way to fix it. For example, a pretty typical problem for products is that new users have no idea how to get started.

There are dozens of ways to fix this. You could do a tutorial, a video, a webinar, a walk-through, inline callouts, tooltips, or contextual help messages, for example. Hell, if you have very few users who are each paying a huge amount of money, you could go to each customer's house personally and teach him how to use it.

This is the time to get all those different options on the table for further evaluation.

As I'm sure you've been told, this is not the time to shoot down people's ideas. In our help example, you don't want to ignore the person in the corner saying things like, "What if Ryan Gosling were to answer all of our support questions?" even if you feel it's not the most cost-efficient method of helping users.

Perhaps the most important thing to consider about brainstorming is that it should be a very, very, very short process. People who love this part of the job will try to suck you into four-hour "strategy" meetings that are really thinly veiled brainstorming meetings.

Don't do it. If you're just brainstorming, and not starting arguments over every stupid idea (and let's face it, some ideas are really stupid, no matter what they tell you in brainstorming school), you will run out of ideas very quickly.

Start the session by clearly stating the user problem and the reason you are choosing to solve it. Explain how you will measure the success of the experiment. Then have everybody write down their ideas in a sentence or two. Go around the room, have people read their ideas, write them on the whiteboard, and don't let people discuss beyond clarifying certain specifics about the idea.

Depending on the types of ideas that people are presenting, you may want to start grouping ideas in a way that makes sense to you. Feel free to group by things like which metric will be affected, ease of implementation, or customer problem that you're solving. Those can all be helpful in deciding what's most important to do next.

Try to do this in under 15 minutes. Seriously. If it takes much longer than that, you're including too many people or talking about too many things.

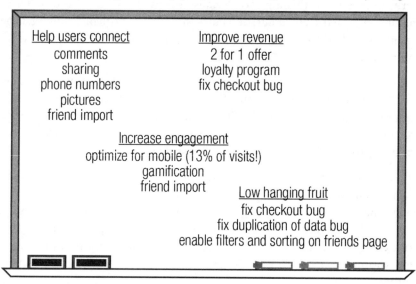

Figure 5-2. This part should not take more than 15 minutes

Feel free to ask people at the end whether they feel strongly about a particular solution they'd like to try, but whatever you do, don't take a vote. This is an opportunity to get some new ideas, not some stupid experiment in democratic government.

When Is It Safe to Skip This?

I just said you can do this in 15 minutes. Why would you skip it? The truth is, by continually checking in with your team and the stakeholders, you're going to save yourself time in the long run, because they will catch mistakes and problems that you might miss.

Tool 5: Make a Decision

Welcome to the hardest part of the design process. You need to pick something to try. If you can't make hard decisions and then stick to them for at least as long as it takes to prove whether you were right or wrong, you are going to need to change careers, because this is a necessary skill.

But don't fret. I'm not going to send you into the wilderness empty-handed. I'm going to remind you of a very important calculation called ROI—return on investment.

Every possible solution has an expected cost and an expected return. Of course, your expectations of both things are probably completely wrong, but you have to do this anyway, because you will get better and better at making expected ROI calculations as you do more of them. Don't get me wrong. You'll still probably suck at them, but you'll suck less, and it's a useful exercise.

A good way to do this is to create a simple graph with x- and y-axes. Label one "Expected Return" and one "Expected Cost." Then put all your different features on the graph. While you won't be able to truly estimate the exact cost of every different feature, it's pretty easy to estimate which ones are going to take far more time or engineering effort.

Oh, in case you're thinking to yourself that you don't really know how to estimate engineering effort, this might be a good time to mention that you should have someone from engineering involved in this effort. Same goes for any of the other people in your company who might be affected by your changes. That can be marketing, customer service, sales, or anyone else who needs to weigh in on unexpected costs or benefits of particular features.

Again, none of those people are going to vote on the right decision to be made. What they will do is provide enough information about the real expected costs and benefits of each feature so you can make the decision.

An important thing to keep in mind during this process is that, depending on the size and complexity of your company, this process may have to be quite iterative. Engineering may not have enough information at this point to commit to a solid estimate. Marketing may be able to give only a rough estimate of what sort of support they'll need for the new feature. Sales may have things they need added to make the feature really effective for them.

That's OK. You don't need to know absolutely everything about the feature at this point. You just need to get everybody thinking about the decision as early as possible so that, as problems do arise, you'll have more people on your team to catch them and fix them.

When Is It Safe to Skip This?

Never. Never ever ever ever ever. You must make a decision. There is nothing I see more often at failing startups than a fundamental inability to make a damn decision. If you have done your research and involved your team, you are ready to make a decision, even if you don't know it's the right one.

Don't worry. You're going to validate whether this is the right idea or not. But first you have to pick a direction to go in.

Tool 6: (In)Validate the Approach

OK, this section should have been titled "(In)Validate the Approach When Possible and Financially Worthwhile," but it looked weird.

The reason this is here is because the next few tools can take some time. While understanding the problem and getting your team on board are not really negotiable parts of the design process, everything that follows this can be avoided with one easy trick: Invalidate your idea.

"What's that?" you say. "Why would I want to invalidate my idea?" The simple answer is because if you can prove that you're about to make a huge mistake, it's very possible for you to avoid making it. And, yes, even if you've used all the tools provided to you so far in the chapter, you could still be making a huge mistake.

Here's an example. Imagine you're working on an e-commerce company that sells gadgets. Now imagine you've spent a lot of time talking to your users, and you realize that one of the biggest reasons people don't buy gadgets is they feel like they already have too many they don't use. Furthermore, imagine that another common reason people don't buy new gadgets is price.

You and your team might reasonably come to the conclusion that a good solution to both of these problems would be to allow people to resell their own gadgets in order to get new ones. This would be a perfectly reasonable hypothesis about a way to fix a known problem.

What you want to do next is figure out if the hypothesis is wrong. Too often, the solution to a problem seems so obvious to us, but it simply fails to catch on with users. Think of how much time you would waste implementing an entire system allowing users to sell their own gadgets on your site if none of them actually wanted to sell any.

I talk in the next chapter about Feature Stubs, and that's what you might want to do here. Design the smallest possible thing that you can that might invalidate your hypothesis. In this example, that might be a Sell Your Gadget button in an obvious place in your product that counts the number of times people click it and gives a nice message saying the feature isn't fully implemented yet. If nobody ever clicks the button, it's a great signal that you don't want to build the full version of the feature, at least until you understand the problem or the market better.

The reason this is so important is that every failed feature you don't build saves you money and time so that you can build more features that are more likely to succeed.

When Is It Safe to Skip This?

There are some features or changes that simply take more time to validate than they do to build. Before you implement a fake feature or come up with some other ingenious test to see if you're going in the right direction, ask yourself how long the feature will take to build and how long it will take to test in this manner. If it's almost as fast to just build it and test it in production, then feel free to do that.

Tool 7: Sketch a Few Approaches

I'm a big fan of starting to sketch at this point in the design process. You'll note we're on Tool 7 here.

Unfortunately, this is where a lot of folks start the design process. The thing is, once you start sketching, you can have a tendency to focus on the details—where a button goes, what pieces of the interface belong together, how much text will be necessary.

That's OK to do on Tool 7. You're ready for it now. You probably already have a picture of what you want to design in your head.

Every designer I've talked to has a different preferred way of "sketching." I'm going to give you mine, but you may end up liking a different method. That's fine. The most important things about sketching are that it's quick and that it's disposable. This is your chance to try out a few different versions of your new feature or product.

Because you're going to want to create several different versions of your idea quickly, and because you're going to want to iterate quickly on your ideas, I suggest you use a sketching tool like Balsamiq or OmniGraffle. There are about a dozen others. Those are the two I use. They are easy to learn, and they produce things at a high enough fidelity to get your point across.

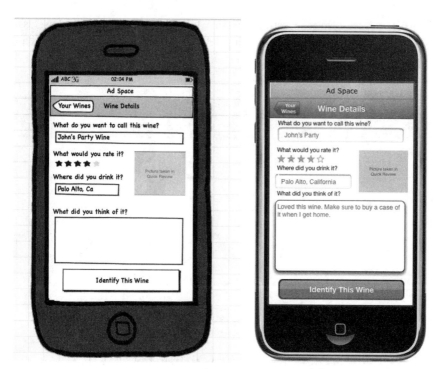

Figure 5-3. Same sketch, different fidelities

Your goal with sketching is to start to work out things like what elements belong on a screen and what pieces belong together. For example, if you're creating a product page to sell something, you're almost certainly going to want a picture of the thing you're selling, a buy button, and a price. Those things should probably be pretty close together. Other than that, though, you have a lot of directions you could go.

Because sketching is so quick, it's a great time to do things like work out the flows of basic tasks. Often people forget that what they are sketching is almost certainly not a static thing. It has actions and states. Buttons can be pressed. Forms can be filled in, sometimes incorrectly. When you're sketching, it's a good time to get through as many of the different states as possible to make sure that they can all be handled.

Whenever you sketch an interactive element, make sure you're adding a screen or a note about what happens when somebody interacts with that element. If you add a drop-down list, think through what might be in that drop-down list.

Too often I see "sketches" that are so vague as to be completely useless. While these are technically sketches, they are not particularly useful in helping you to work out how a user will interact with your product. And that's really the point of sketching.

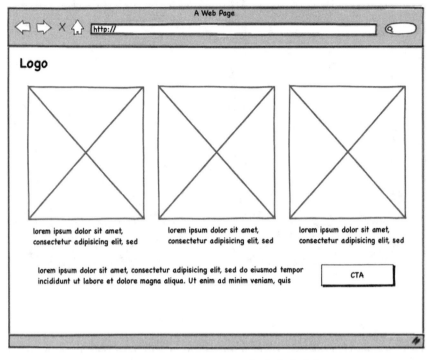

Figure 5-4. Not particularly helpful

Once you have several versions of your sketches produced, it's time to make a few more decisions. The most important decision is which ones to move forward with, since it's very rarely a good idea to move forward with three or four completely different designs, unless you have a lot of bored engineers and an entire testing system already set up to A/B test all the versions against one another.

For most of us with limited resources, it's generally best to pick one or two sketches that we think are most likely to fix the problems we observed in the initial research. The best way to do this is to get your sketches in front of actual users again.

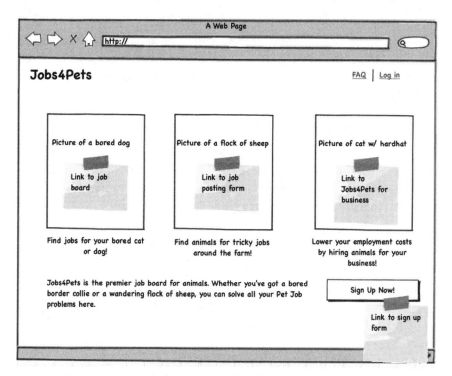

Figure 5-5. Including text and calls-to-action makes this sketch useful

Your goal for testing your sketches with users isn't to try to understand the usability of the design, it's to understand, overall, whether potential users get what the product is and can find the starting point for all of their most important tasks.

Let's look at an example. Imagine that you've created a few sketches of a new e-commerce product page. You know that the most important things for people to do on this page are to buy the product or to share the product with friends. Show the sketches to some strangers, preferably on a computer. Ask the following questions:

- What do you think this screen is for?

- How would you buy something?

- Imagine that you think it would be perfect for a friend. How would you share it with that friend?

Don't forget to mix up the order in which you show people the sketches, so everybody doesn't see the same sketch first.

If, after you've done this four or five times, nobody is having any trouble understanding any of the sketches, then feel free to pick your favorite and move on. If, on the other hand, everybody is having trouble with all the sketches, pay close attention to where people are looking and try a few new sketches. Repeat.

When Is It Safe to Skip This?

When you're making a change that is easier to communicate or test in another way, you don't need to create a sketch. For example, if you're making a simple visual design change, it might be faster or more efficient to show the change in Photoshop or even in HTML and CSS.

In other cases, you may be making major changes to your product that you know will require fully interactive prototypes, and you may want to begin your design process with one of those.

Don't sketch for the sake of sketching. Sketch because it helps you to develop and communicate your design ideas quickly. And if it's not going to do that, then you're welcome to skip it.

Tool 8: Create Interactive Prototypes

I'm a huge fan of interactive prototypes, but there's often some confusion about what those are. Let's be clear: When I say interactive prototypes, I don't mean something created in PowerPoint that somebody could kind of click through. I mean a full-scale, working prototype that allows users to explore and feel like they're accomplishing tasks.

Unsurprisingly, it's a little hard to illustrate what I mean in a book, but interactive wireframes have things like widgets that respond to users and animations that work and forms that users can fill in. They are interactive enough for users to make mistakes and recover from them. They are realistic enough that users often think they're just an ugly, boring, nonvisually designed version of the real product.

Here's the problem with interactive prototypes: They take a long time to build. I mean, they don't take as long to build as a real product, because often they have a rudimentary visual design and no backend to speak of. For example, you might have an interactive prototype that lets a user feel like he was purchasing a product but didn't actually process a payment or ship him anything.

In general, they are wonderful for figuring out what's confusing or hard to use about your product before you write a lot of code. They also serve as a fantastic tool for communicating to engineers exactly what you want them to build.

For example, imagine that you are building that checkout flow. Maybe you want parts of the interface to be shown only after a user performs a specific task. Instead of writing a document that explains in detail everything that you want to have happen, you simply include it in the prototype. Or maybe you want a particular animation to happen when a user presses a button. You can show exactly the style, speed, and behavior of the animation in your prototype.

So, now that you know all the wonderful reasons you'd want to build an interactive prototype, you have to decide whether it's worth spending the time to do so. There are a few criteria you should use to make this decision.

First, is it a complex interaction? Any time you have a sequence of steps where a user needs to make a number of choices, it's probably worth it to do a prototype. Multiple steps mean multiple chances for users to get lost or to get something wrong, and the more complex or potentially confusing an interaction, the more important it is to prototype it.

Second, will it take awhile to build and, more importantly, will it take awhile to fix if you get it wrong? One of the biggest reasons people give for not making prototypes is that they simply don't have the time, but if it's a big, complicated interaction that can take a few days to build, it can also take days to fix if there's something particularly confusing about it. On the other hand, if an engineer can build the entire working feature in about the same time it would take me to build an entire prototype, I'll generally err on the side of just building and testing it in production.

Third, how often do you make changes to your product? If you're serious about being Lean, hopefully you practice continuous deployment, so you can ship a fix immediately rather than waiting for weeks for a new version of the product, but not everybody's work environment is like that. If you're building something that simply can't be changed on the fly, like a physical product or a heavily regulated piece of software, then interactive prototypes are crucial for finding as many problems as possible before you ship.

The last question to ask yourself before you build the interactive prototype is whether it will help you, as the designer or product owner, figure out important things about the design. More often than you'd think, the answer to this question will be a resounding yes.

You see, if you're designing something interactive, you need to design it to be...well...interactive. Too often, designers design screens in something like Photoshop or Illustrator, as if screens were the end product. But screens aren't the end product. Screens are snapshots of particular states that a user might encounter in your product.

For example, a single screen in a checkout flow could have all sorts of states. It could have multiple types of errors, or a user could back out of the checkout flow and come back to it, or she could abandon the checkout flow altogether, or she could click through to read more about the terms of service. By creating an interactive prototype, the designer is forced to think through every single interaction on the screen and the different states that could be caused by different types of input.

Which brings us to a very important question: How should you create your interactive prototypes? Well, here again I tend to differ from other designers. I make my interactive prototypes in HTML, JavaScript, and CSS. Knowing enough programming to create prototypes means that I have a lot of flexibility in what I can design. I'm not limited by the capabilities of prototyping tools.

But, by all means, if you're an absolute whiz with some other type of tool, like Axure or Flash, that really allows you to create a fully interactive experience, use that.

When Is It Safe to Skip This?

If you're designing something very simple, quick, and not highly interactive, by all means, skip the interactive prototype. I will always skip the prototypes on things like landing pages with a single call-to-action; messaging changes; and small, new features with very little interactivity.

Deciding whether or not to make an interactive prototype is essentially an ROI question. If an engineer can build and release a feature for testing in less time than it would take to build a prototype, often it makes no sense to bother with one. However, if you stand to lose significant time, revenue, or customers by releasing a major change without truly understanding the usability of the feature, building and testing an interactive prototype can be a lifesaver.

Tool 9: Test and Iterate

OK, now we're on the last tool. Pretty exciting! You're almost done! Oh, except for the part where you have to test and go back and do everything all over again.

If you truly think that the very first thing you design will be completely perfect and not require any changes, you are either delusional or you are a better designer than anybody I've ever met. No, I take that back. You're totally delusional.

One of the major differences between Lean and other methodologies is the extreme importance of iteration. You see, if you really do crank out an absolutely perfect design the first time around, you are spending way too much time up front.

Build things, prototype things, and get things in front of users as quickly as possible to find out what they like and what they hate and what they find horribly confusing. Then fix the problems and add things you think they'll like and keep doing that until you've got a feature that people are excited about.

I know that nine tools seems like a lot to use over and over, but you'll find that they go very quickly once you realize that you don't have to get everything absolutely perfect the first time.

When Is It Safe to Skip This?

I can't believe you even asked this question. I'm ashamed of you.

Promise me that you will never skip testing or iteration. I mean it.

Loosely Related Rant: Give the Users What They Really Want

In the past, I've tried to teach startups how to do their own user research and design. I've noticed that I teach a lot of the same things over and over again, since there are a few things about research that seem to be especially difficult for new folks.

One of the most common problems, and possibly the toughest one to overcome, is the tendency to accept solutions from users without understanding the underlying problem.

In other words, a user says, "I want X feature," and instead of learning why she wants that feature, entrepreneurs and product owners tend to write down, "Users want X feature" and then move on.

This is a huge issue with novices performing research. When you do this, you are letting your users design your product for you, and this is bad because, in general, users are terrible at design.

Ooh! An Example!

I participated in some user research for a company with an expensive set of products and services. Users coming to the company's website were looking for information so they could properly evaluate which set of products and services was right for them. Typically, users ended up buying a custom package of products and services.

One thing we heard from several users was that they really wanted more case studies. Case studies, they said, were extremely helpful.

Now, if you're conducting user research, and a customer tells you that he wants case studies, this might sound like a great idea.

Unfortunately, the user has just presented you with a solution, not a problem. The reason that this is important is that, based on what the actual underlying problem is, there might be several better solutions available to you.

When we followed up on users' requests for case studies with the question, "Why do you want to see case studies?" we got three different answers. Interestingly, the users asking for case studies were trying to solve entirely different problems. But were case studies really the best solution for all three problems?

These were the responses along with some analysis.

> *"I want to know what other companies similar to mine are doing so that I have a good idea of what I should buy."*

The first user's "problem" was that he didn't know how to pick the optimal collection of products for his company. This is a choice problem. It's like when you're trying to buy a new home theater system, and you have to make a bunch of interrelated decisions about very expensive items that you probably don't know much about.

While case studies can certainly be helpful in these instances, it's often more effective to solve choice problems with some sort of recommendation engine or a selection of preset packages.

Both of these quickly help the user understand what the right selection is for him rather than just give him a long explanation of how somebody else found a good solution that might or might not be applicable to the user.

> *"I want to know what sorts of benefits other companies got from the purchase so I can tell whether it's worth buying."*

The second user's "problem" was that he wanted to make sure he was getting a good value for his money. This is a metrics problem. It's like when you're trying to figure out if it's worth it to buy the more expensive stereo system. You need to understand exactly what you're getting for your money with each system and then balance the benefits versus the cost.

This problem might have been solved by a price matrix showing exactly what benefits were offered for different products. Alternatively, it would be faster and more effective to display only the pertinent part of the case studies on the product description page—for example, "Customers saw an average of 35% increase in revenue six months after installing this product."

By boiling this down to only the parts of the case study that are important to the user, it gives you more flexibility to show this information—statistics, metrics, etc.—in more prominent and pertinent places on the site. This actually increases the impact of these numbers and improves the chance that people will see them.

> *"I want to see what other sorts of companies you work with so that I can decide whether you have a reputable company."*

The third user's "problem" was that he hadn't ever heard of the company selling the products. Since they were expensive products, he wanted the reassurance that companies he had heard of were already clients. This is a social proof problem. It's like when you're trying to pick somebody to put a new roof on your house, so you ask your friends for recommendations.

His actual problem could have been solved a lot quicker with a carousel of short client testimonials. Why go to all the trouble of writing up several big case studies when all the user cares about is seeing a Google logo in your client list?

Why this matters

This shouldn't come as a surprise to any of you, but users ask for things they're familiar with, not necessarily what would be best for them. If a user has seen something like case studies before, then when he thinks about the value he got from case studies, he's going to ask for more of the same. He's not necessarily going to just ask for the part of the case study that was most pertinent to him.

The problem with this is that many people who might also find certain parts of case studies compelling won't bother to read them because case studies can be quite long or because the user doesn't think that the particular case study applies to him.

Obviously, this is applicable to a lot more than case studies. For example, I recently saw a very similar situation from buyers and sellers in a social marketplace asking for a "reputation system" when what they really wanted was some sort of reassurance that they wouldn't get ripped off. I could name a dozen other examples.

The takeaway is that, when somebody asks you for a feature, you need to follow up with questions about why she wants the feature, even when you think you already know the answer!

Once you know what the problems really are, you can go about solving them in the most efficient, effective way, rather than the way the user just happened to think of during the conversation.

Instead of just building what the user asks for, build something that solves the user's real problem. As an added bonus, you might end up building a smaller, easier feature than the one the user asked for.

Go Do This Now!

- Write some stories: Try breaking down a current feature into a complete set of user stories.

- Do some sketching: Try taking the user stories and creating three rough sketches of how one of the screens might look. If that goes well, THEN sketch all the screens for the feature.

- Learn what your users really want: Try looking at a feature that's commonly requested by users and figuring out what problem they're trying to solve.

CHAPTER 6

Just Enough Design

In this chapter:

- Learn several important tips for designing the right stuff faster.

- Get tools that give you real insight into whether or not you should build a feature.

- Understand how to tell necessary features from nice-to-have features.

Sorry, still not going to teach you how to be a brilliant designer. Instead, I'm going to teach you something just as important: when not to design. If the previous chapter was about the fundamentals you need to know in order to design something, this chapter is about ways to figure out when not to jump into the design process at all.

Remember, it is important to know how to design things, but it's just as important to know when not to design anything. Avoiding extra work isn't lazy. It's smart. It means you'll have more time to do great design work on the things that matter.

You see, the beauty of the Lean methodology is that it forces you to get rid of many of your old, ingrained habits that slowed you down and made you design things that never got built or build things that never got used.

Lean UX is often about doing just enough design. Please note that the word "enough" is pretty important here. Just enough design doesn't mean crappy design or hard-to-use design. Just enough design means doing what you need to do to learn what you want to learn.

Design the Necessary, Not the Neat

Designers design. It's right there in the job title. The problem is that we can overdesign. We can spend a lot of time focusing on the details and the vision and a lot of other things that don't directly relate to solving a problem.

Look, I just explained that you need to figure out how you're going to test to see whether your design change actually made a measurable difference to your business. Now let's talk about making sure you're only making design changes that make a measurable difference to your business.

Those two things are different. Seriously.

Whether you're a trained designer or somebody who just needs to know enough design to get your product in front of users, you're going to have to stop thinking about design primarily as a way to make things beautiful or cool or interesting. Your goal for this type of design is to make things easy, obvious, and useful.

The way to do that is to strip out everything that isn't necessary to validate your hypothesis or to move your key metric.

This is a tough concept to get, so let's look at some examples, both good and bad. Have you bought anything at Amazon recently? Oh wait. You're human, so probably.

Have you noticed all the stuff it has on its product pages? There's a lot of it. It has recommendations and reviews and other places to buy and descriptions and ratings and...about a million other things. It also sells a couple of versions of virtually every product known to mankind.

Figure 6-1. I've been looking for this everywhere!

Because of the way Amazon creates its product, I have a fairly high certainty that each of those things helps it sell more products. I also know, because I was around at the time, that it didn't have most of that stuff when it started selling books back in the prehistoric era of the Internet.

That's the thing. Each of those elements it's imagined and designed and built and tested took a really long time to imagine, design, build, and test. If you decide to build a product page with all that stuff on it, you'd better be independently wealthy, because that shit's going to take awhile.

What You Should Do Instead

Let's imagine that you are going to sell something. What do you need to validate whether you can sell that thing?

Well, you need all of this:

- Reasons a person might want to buy the thing

- A way for people to indicate that they might want to buy the thing

- Enough people to conduct an experiment to see how many people actually want to buy the thing

Would it be great if people could also comment on the thing they bought? Sure! Will that make people buy the thing if they weren't planning to buy it previously? Unlikely. How about ratings on the thing? Will those significantly affect the number of people who buy? Hard to say. Or what if you showed people more things to buy? That could increase the number of things they buy.

Are any of those things absolutely necessary to test whether people will buy something from you? Nope.

You see, you need to design and build the things that are absolutely necessary first. In this case, give people something they might want to buy and give them a way to buy it. The other things are nice to have, but they are not absolutely, critically necessary for validation of your assumption.

They're also getting in the way of you launching the necessary stuff and starting to get people buying things from you.

When you're designing a new feature, for example a product page where people can buy things, try to strip it down to only the most necessary parts. Maybe, for you, comments are absolutely necessary, because your entire model is based on personal referrals of products. Maybe ratings are the critical element because your idea is that professional ratings increase intent to purchase.

Regardless, you need to find, design, and build everything that is absolutely necessary first and no more. Because if the necessary is an abysmal failure, there's an excellent chance that slapping on the nice-to-have won't save it.

Here's Another Example

I talked with some people from a company that had a fairly successful product. They wanted to add a new feature to their product. They spent a lot of time discussing how the feature would work, what it would do for users, how users would interact with it, and all the other sorts of conversations you tend to see around exciting new features.

Then they got to a key question: How would users access the feature?

They decided that the feature was important enough to include in their main navigation. Unfortunately, there wasn't any place that their new feature fit nicely.

They decided they would need to redesign their entire main navigation for the product. This, of course, meant that all the other small changes they'd been saving for the main navigation had to go into this redesign. Also, they'd have to do a full visual redesign of the main navigation. Oh, and if they were doing a full visual redesign of the navigation, obviously they'd have to update the visual design on the rest of the application to match.

Did I mention that, when they finally launched the new feature, users didn't care about it? It failed to move a single metric, and the company eventually pulled it entirely.

What They Should Have Done

They should have done pretty much anything else. The whole experience was incredibly expensive and demoralizing, and I'd like to say it's the only time I've ever seen it happen, but that would be a lie.

The most important thing they failed to do was to validate the feature itself before changing the entire site to accommodate it.

They could have done this in a number of ways:

- They could have done more customer validation before they created the feature to see if the feature would solve a real customer pain point.

- They could have added the feature and advertised it directly to a small percentage of their users and asked them explicitly to try it out and give feedback.

- They could have added access to the feature from someplace that wasn't the main navigation, but that was still accessible to users, and tested with it there.

- They could have just made small changes to the current main navigation in order to fit the feature in with the idea that they would go back and improve the display in the main navigation later if the feature was a hit.

- They could have used what I call a Feature Stub. That's next.

Build a Feature Stub

OK, that last example depressed me. Let's look at a nice example of the right amount of design. This is probably the most commonly used trick in the Lean UX arsenal. It's wonderful, because it allows you to test a feature without building anything at all! What could be faster than that?

I often consult with companies that are considering selling a particular item or package or feature. For example, I was talking to a company that wanted to start charging for certain features on its free product.

When we spoke, they immediately started talking about things like whether they should charge a one-time fee or a subscription, whether they should allow a free trial, and what payments they should accept. They told me that they wanted me to design the payment flow so that users would be more likely to buy the upgrade.

I stopped and asked what I think is a reasonably important question: Do you have any evidence that anybody will buy this thing at all?

The reason I asked was that all of the questions they were trying to answer are hard to solve, design, and build. Despite the sheer number of things being bought and sold on the Internet, great payment flows can still be tricky. Also, did you know that integrating with payment systems is the leading cause of Developer Rage Syndrome, which is a syndrome I just totally made up? True story.

The first step was to validate whether anybody wanted to pay for any part of the company's free system. Here is the design that you need to start testing that assumption: a button that says Upgrade and a static page with a price and a couple of features you might offer when the user upgrades.

You also need a way on the backend to calculate the number of people who click on that button and a way to A/B test how changing the price and benefit statements affect conversion. These are far easier to build than an entire payment system and flow. Besides, you should really have the ability to A/B test this kind of stuff anyway.

What Does This Have to Do with Design?

OK, I admit it. This doesn't seem to have a lot to do with great design. It's more like avoiding design. But a huge component of great design is spending the time on the stuff that's important and not wasting time on the things that aren't going to work.

If you like, think of it as experiment design. Your job is to design the best possible experiment to validate or invalidate your hypothesis.

Maybe your hypothesis is that people will love your new feature or will be willing to pay for certain parts of your system. Whatever it is, do as little work as humanly possible to figure out if that's true, because you're going to have a whole hell of a lot of work to do once you figure out that people desperately want whatever you're selling.

Build a Wizard of Oz Feature

When I was consulting, I worked with a company called Food on the Table. Now, Food on the Table has a product that helps people plan their meals around whatever is on sale at their local grocery store. At the time I write this, they have the daily sale information from literally thousands of grocery stores all over the United States.

It's a great idea. It's also a giant pain in the ass to implement. After all, you have to have some way to collect all that information from all those grocery stores in order to share with users. You also have to have an easy-to-use onboarding flow to gather information from people about where they shop and what food they like.

So they didn't do that. At least, they didn't do it at first. Instead, they decided they needed to learn more about how people shop and whether people would be interested in the product they wanted to build.

Instead of doing all the design and engineering work to build the product for everybody all at once, they got a few potential customers and did the work manually. That's right. Instead of spending the first few weeks getting sale data and building a user interface, they went to the store, got the sale circulars, and sat down with some potential users to help them plan a meal. There was no design or engineering involved at all.

Now, it turned out that people loved the idea, so that's when they decided to go ahead and start designing and building. But if people had hated the idea, even when they had somebody literally sitting down with them and helping them plan their meals for free, would there really have been any point to building the rest of the product? Probably not.

We call this the Wizard of Oz feature or sometimes a concierge service, and tons of companies use it all the time. Here are some other examples of great Wizard of Oz features:

- Using crowdsourcing or something like Mechanical Turk to collect data rather than writing code to gather it.

- Packing and shipping products yourself rather than integrating with a distribution center.

- Approving orders manually rather than trying to build an entire fraud detection system to make sure that you have valid orders. Once again, this gives you a way to avoid design entirely, because avoiding wasted design is one of the best ways to save time in the entire universe.

Solve Only the Important Problems

First, let me tell you a story about a very small bug we encountered at Food on the Table, one that was having a pretty big effect on metrics.

As I mentioned before, Food on the Table lets users create meal plans based on what's for sale at their local grocery stores. There was a call-to-action button that allowed a user to add a meal to her meal plan.

When the company tested the button locally, it all worked perfectly. Users pushed the button and the meal was added. Worked every time.

The problem came when users with slower connections or slower computers pushed the button. In many of those cases, when users pushed the button, there was a delay of up to a few seconds. What this meant was the user would push the button, but nothing would appear to be happening. She would then push the button several more times, hoping to make something happen. When the button clicks registered in the UI, the user would have added the meal to the meal plan several times, which was clearly not her intention.

We discovered this bug quickly in observational testing. It was happening to enough people that we were fairly certain it was negatively affecting key metrics, especially for new users.

Then we needed to figure out how to fix it. This is where the concept of "as little design as possible" came in.

Now, as you can imagine, there are lots of ways to fix this problem. The immediate engineering response might be to reduce the latency on the button so that the button clicks were recorded faster. Anybody who's ever written any code will recognize this as potentially a Very Hard Problem.

A different approach might be to simply have the user interface reflect the change the user made without waiting for a response from the server. This is fraught with dangers, of course, because it can allow what the user sees to get out of sync with what's in the database.

I could give you five or six other possible solutions, but the very simple one that we came up with was simply to show a working state spinner on the disabled button until the process finished. Since the wait was never more than a few seconds, people were perfectly content to wait while their choice was recorded.

Why do I bother to tell this story? Well, it's important to realize that this solution worked in this particular case for a lot of reasons. For example, users were typically adding only three to five meals to their meal plans at a time. Waiting a few seconds for each one to be added did not significantly affect their total time performing the task. If it was a task they had to repeat hundreds of times, the three-second pause would have become a problem.

That's the important thing to remember here. If all goes well, over the course of your product's life, you will make far more of these small, iterative changes than you will big, sweeping changes. It's important to have a process for figuring out the smallest possible change you can make that is appropriate to your situation.

How You Can Do It Right Now

Find a bug you want to fix. Not a typo-type bug. Something that is clearly affecting your metrics but that may not have an absolutely obvious fix. This could be a user-experience bug, like "Nobody knows how to share a file," or a technology bug, like "It takes five minutes to upload a profile picture."

The first step is to determine if it's worth fixing at all.

To do that, try to answer the following questions:

- Who is this problem affecting?
- How often does it affect them?
- Which key metric is it potentially damaging?

If it's affecting important users a decent percentage of the time and negatively affecting a key metric, it's certainly worth fixing. If it's two of the three, it's still probably worth fixing. The point is, not all bugs need to be fixed, but too many serious bugs can create an extremely negative experience for your users.

The next step is to find the key problem it's causing for users. Just "not behaving as expected" isn't necessarily the issue. It's got to be getting in the way of people using your product successfully.

The best way to really understand a problem is, of course, to see it in action. Get some real users to show you the problem themselves on their own computers or devices. Understand what the bug is, when people are encountering it, and what it's preventing them from doing.

Now—and this is the tricky design part—you need to solve the actual problem that the bug is causing. This is where you have to brainstorm some different solutions. The one you select should satisfy two important rules:

1. It should solve the problem that users are having.

2. It should be the best solution that takes the least amount of time.

I can almost hear some of you saying, "But sometimes things that take very little time now can cost time in the future!" That's both true and irrelevant. Try not to solve problems you don't have yet. If you take too long solving this problem, your company may not survive to solve the next one.

This is why in my example we chose to simply display to the user that her button push had been accepted rather than implement the more costly solution of making round trips to the server much faster.

We didn't do the harder thing because we didn't need to. We could solve the main user problem—they pushed the button too many times because they didn't know it worked the first time—by simply letting them know it worked the first time.

This may seem like a lengthy process for something that seems as simple as fixing a bug. And, of course, I'm not in any way advocating that you do this when fixing typos. But anytime there are multiple approaches to fixing a bug, some of those approaches will be faster than others. Spending a little time to find a faster way to solve a problem saves you time in the end.

The other thing you may notice I didn't tell you to do was extensive prototyping and user testing of the bug fix. There are lots of kinds of design changes where these are necessary. This type of UI bug fix, as long as the user problem is well enough understood ahead of time, tends not to require prototyping or usability testing.

Loosely Related Rant: Stop Worrying About the Cup Holders

Every startup I've ever talked to has too few resources. Programmers, money, marketing...you name it, startups don't have enough of it.

When you don't have enough resources, prioritization becomes even more important. You don't have the luxury to execute every single great idea you have. You need to pick and choose, and the life of your company depends on choosing wisely.

Why is it that so many startups work so hard on the wrong stuff?

By "the wrong stuff" I mean, of course, stuff that doesn't move a key metric—projects that don't convert people into new users or increase revenue or drive retention. And it's especially problematic for new startups, since they are often missing really important features that would drive all those key metrics.

It's as if they had a car without any brakes, and they're worried about building the perfect cup holder.

For some reason, when you're in the middle of choosing features for your product, it can be really hard to distinguish between brakes and cup holders. How do you do it?

You need to start by asking (and answering) two simple questions:

- What problem is this solving?
- How important is this problem in relation to the other problems I have to solve?

To accurately answer these questions, it helps to be able to identify some things that frequently get worked on that just don't have that big of a return. So what does a cup-holder project look like? It often looks like the following things.

Visual Design

Visual design can be incredibly important, but 9 times out of 10, it's a cup holder. Obviously colors, fonts, and layout can affect things like conversion, but it's typically an optimization of conversion rather than a conversion driver.

For example, the fact that you allow users to buy things on your website at all has a much bigger impact on revenue than the color of the buy button. Maybe that's an extreme example, but I've seen too many companies spending time quibbling over the visual design of incredibly important features, which just ends up delaying the release of these features.

Go ahead. Make your site pretty. Some of that visual improvement may even contribute to key metrics. But every time you put off releasing a feature in order to make sure you've got exactly the right gradient, ask yourself, "Am I redesigning a cup holder here, or am I turbocharging the engine?"

Retention Features

Retention is a super important metric. You should absolutely think about retaining your users—once you have users.

Far too many people start worrying about having great retention features long before they have any users to retain. Having 100% retention is a wonderful thing, but if your acquisition and activation metrics are too low, you could find yourself retaining one really happy user until you go out of business.

Before you spend a lot of time working on rewards for super users, ask yourself if you're ready for that yet. Remember, great cup-holder design can make people who already own the car incredibly happy, but you've got to get them to buy it first, and nobody ever bought a junker for the cup holders.

Animations

I am not anti-animation. In fact, sometimes a great animation or other similar detail in a design can make a feature great. Sometimes a well-designed animation can reduce confusion and make a feature easy to use.

The problem is, you have to figure out if the animation you're adding is going to make your feature significantly more usable or just a little cooler.

As a general rule, if you have to choose between usable and cool, choose usable first. I'm not saying you shouldn't try to make your product cool. You absolutely should. But animations can take a disproportionate amount of time and resources to get right, and unless they're adding something really significant to your interface, you may be better served leaving them until later.

"But wait," a legion of designers is screaming. "We shouldn't have to choose between usable and cool! Apple doesn't choose between usable and cool! They just release perfect products!"

That's nice. When you've got more money than most first-world governments, you've got fewer resource constraints than startups typically do. Startups make the usable/cool trade-off every day, and I've looked at enough metrics to know that a lot of cool but unusable products get used exactly once and then immediately abandoned because they're too confusing.

This may seem to contradict my point about attracting users first and then worrying about retention, but I'd like to point out that there's a significant difference between solving long-term retention problems and confusing new users so badly that they never come back.

Before you spend a lot of time making your animation work seamlessly in every browser, ask yourself if the return you're getting is really worth the effort, or if you're just building an animated cup holder.

Your Feature Here

I can't name every single project that might be a cup holder. These are just a couple of examples that I've seen repeatedly.

And, frankly, one product's cup holder might be another product's transmission. The only thing that matters is how much of an effect your proposed change might have on key metrics.

As a business, you should be solving the problems that have the biggest chance of ensuring your survival. Cup-holder projects are distractions that take up too much of your time, and it's up to you to make sure that every project you commit to is going to give you a decent return.

If you want to identify the cup holders, make sure you're always asking yourself what problem a feature is solving and how important that problem is compared with all the other problems you could be solving. Cup holders solve the problem of where to put your drink. Brakes solve the problem of how to keep you from smashing into a wall.

Of course, if I got to choose, I'd rather you built me a car that drives itself. Then I can use both hands to hold my drink.

Go Do This Now!

- Be the Wizard: Try running a Wizard of Oz test on a complicated new feature you're considering building.

- Understand your current product: Try looking at usage on each of your product's current features and figuring out which were truly necessary. You might be surprised.

CHAPTER 7

Design Hacks

In this chapter:

- Learn several tricks that will help you pretend to be a designer. (There's more to it than stylish glasses and comically oversized watches.)

- Understand how to take advantage of design patterns to get your own product built faster.

- Learn when to steal, when to borrow, and when to hire a designer.

Nope. This is also not the chapter where I teach you to be a fabulous designer. (Note: None of the chapters are.)

Instead, this is the chapter where I share some easy tricks and tips for designing faster and smarter. If you have little to no experience designing products, this chapter will make it so you don't have to learn absolutely everything from scratch.

Lean UX isn't about doing bad design work. It's about learning as quickly as possible, and it's impossible to learn anything from a really bad design (other than the fact that people typically aren't interested in using things that are really badly designed).

That being said, most Lean companies move a hell of a lot faster than companies you may be used to working for. Sometimes, having a few tricks up your sleeve that help you design faster can be the difference between a great product and a poorly thought out piece of crap. I know which one I'd rather build.

You may feel like some of these design hacks are cheating. I totally understand your concern. Get over it. When I was just starting out, I had a mentor who helpfully explained to me that the most important thing to know is that you will very rarely design anything from scratch.

We borrow, we steal, we "get inspired." Every so often, we come up with one fantastic new feature or way of displaying information that is truly innovative, but those things tend to get layered on top of lots of standard designs that work the way everybody expects them to.

Look, there are visionary designers out there. They break rules and create amazing interfaces that defy all expectations and amaze and delight users.

There are two problems with this sort of designer:

1. Sometimes a design that seems like it's going to be visionary and amazing and groundbreaking is wildly unusable because nobody has ever seen anything like it before.

2. You probably don't have this sort of designer working at your startup.

Now that we've established that you're almost certainly not going to create a completely new way of interacting with absolutely everything in the process of building your product, let me reassure you of an important fact about design: The vast majority of interactions don't require anything visionary or groundbreaking or amazing. They require something usable and simple and clear.

The other incredibly important fact about design is that there's an excellent chance that somebody else has done something similar to what you want to do.

I'm not telling you to outright steal all of somebody else's work. Not only is this unethical, but it's actually a bad way to create a product, because hopefully nobody else is doing exactly what you're doing.

What I am telling you is that if you are trying to build a user interface for something like comments, you should probably take a look around the Web because there are a huge number of examples, both wonderful and terrible, that you can learn from.

Figure 7-1. Different needs call for different styles

Now, let's imagine that you do want to add some comment-type things to your product. I'll take you on a little tour of all the things you can do to come up with a great comments interface that fits your product. This example is going to be about comments, but assume that this works for any feature or change you want to make. Just follow the process.

Design Patterns

Your first step is to do a little research. Because, you know, you're not the first person to ever think of adding comments.

In fact, if you think you're the first person to ever think of anything, I strongly suggest you type "ui design patterns" into the search engine of your choice and see what happens.

If, for some reason, you suck at Google, why not check out sites called PatternTap (*http://patterntap.com/*) or Mobile Patterns (*http://www.mobile-patterns.com/*) or *Smashing Magazine* (*http://www.smashingmagazine.com/*)? (Full disclosure: I've written a few articles for them.)

The point, as I mentioned before, is not to blatantly rip off anybody else's design. It's to find common patterns and get inspired.

Besides, I promise you that whatever you think you're copying won't stay exactly like that other design if you're really thinking about the problem. What typically happens is that you find lots of interesting ideas that almost fit what you want to do, but not quite.

That's when you need to take all of this and make it your own.

The one thing I want to warn you against is deciding ahead of time which design pattern you're interested in before really understanding the problem you want to solve. I can't tell you how often I heard, "Oh, we want it to look like Facebook/Pinterest/Twitter/Fill in the Blank"...despite the fact that the problem being solved wasn't even remotely related to the problems solved by those interfaces.

Yes, sometimes you may be building something that will benefit from a Pinterest-style layout. Other times you may be building something that would work as a Twitter- or Facebook-style feed. It's OK to draw inspiration from things that are likely to be familiar to your users, but make sure to let the problem you're solving drive the solution you choose.

Once you've spent a little time researching design patterns, you'll likely start to notice patterns on other sites. For example, think about where you would look for a link to login to a website. Did you think "upper-right corner of the screen"? You should have. That's where it goes 90% of the time. There are a thousand little patterns like that in every product you use. You just need to start looking for them.

Competitive Research

If you want to see typical design patterns in the wild, now is the time to check out what your competitors are doing.

The trick with this, as with searching for design patterns, is to really narrow down the feature you're trying to build into its component parts. You see, very often we imagine that whatever we're trying to build is completely novel. And it's true that your product as a whole should be quite different from what everybody else is doing.

But that doesn't mean that the individual pieces of the interface are at all different.

Figure 7-2. Different styles for the same basic action: replying to a comment

We talked about things like comments and logging in as having patterns. But other things have design patterns, as well, and many products have implemented them.

For example, consider the action that you're trying to let your user do. Is she going to be filling in a lot of personal information? Is she picking items from a list? Is she comparing different things she might want to purchase? Is she searching for information about something very specific?

None of these behaviors is specific to any particular product, platform, or activity. You might add something to a list in any number of different contexts—creating a playlist, making a grocery list, figuring out your to-do list for the week.

If your product requires users to add something to a list, make sure to check out the implementation of this in lots of different contexts. It's not that you're going to find the perfect one. It's more about finding things that you like from the different interfaces and seeing if you can combine them into something that fits your users' needs.

Let's go back to our comments example. Perhaps you go through many different sites, all of which implement comments a bit differently. One site lets users give a star rating with the comments. Another site lets users vote comments up and down. A mobile product has a nice feature that limits the amount of typing a user has to do to leave a good comment. Some products allow commenting on other comments, while other products don't.

Your job is to find all the different pieces of these and figure out what combination of them works best for your product. It's going to be quite different depending on the goal you're trying to achieve, but you can create something quite original and useful simply by borrowing pieces from other places.

User Testing the Competition

As we discussed, you're not the first person to design comments. But just because thousands of other people have designed them doesn't necessarily mean that they've all designed them perfectly.

I like to think that other people are making horrible UX mistakes so that I don't have to.

To learn from other people's mistakes, find a few different implementations of something similar to what you want to do. In our example case, you're going to find implementations of comments. Facebook's a good one, obviously, but try to find a few other styles, as well. Maybe find one or two that you personally think are really well designed or that have some features that apply to your product. For example, if you feel like you need a product rating system, look for comment systems that incorporate various types of rating systems.

Now just do some very basic usability testing on them. This is a great time to use a remote usability testing service like UserTesting.com. Watch four or five people performing tasks with four or five different implementations of the feature you're thinking of implementing.

Obviously, you don't need the competitors to be actual competitors. For example, you could test commenting on shopping sites, even if you're adding comments to a social sharing app. You will want to test on the appropriate platform, though. Usability testing a website doesn't do you much good if you're designing an iPhone app.

If you honestly can't find anything that is at all remotely like the thing you think you're designing, either you're trying too hard to be innovative or you're thinking too literally. For example, gathering a user's personal data requires very similar tactics whether you're gathering it in order to help him do his taxes or to get his medical records.

Why would you bother learning what other people are doing wrong? Well, the great thing about watching people use other types of software is that you start to see all the things that are really broken and hard to use. That means you can avoid making the same mistakes.

I was working for a company that had a very large catalog of products. One of the biggest complaints from users was that they had a hard time finding the things they were looking for. Instead of trying to solve this problem from scratch, we ran usability tests on several different large catalog shopping sites and had users try to find products from each one.

We learned that certain kinds of filters and sorting worked better than others for very large catalogs of products. We also learned where users tended to look for those features. In fact, we found dozens of major usability problems with some of the biggest catalog sites on the Web—sites that you'd really think would know better.

When we launched our own version of a catalog, people were able to find products much more easily, mostly because we hadn't made common mistakes.

Consistency

This one's not so much a hack as it is something we all need to spend more time thinking about. But don't underestimate the enormous effect it can have on making your product much more professional and usable.

Worry less about making your product's interface innovative and cool and elegant, and spend more time worrying about making your product consistent.

For example, imagine you're building a web application. How many different top-level navigational layouts should you have? If your answer is anything other than "one," then you need to think about how many products you're actually building.

This is a common problem that causes users to get incredibly lost. It tends to happen when products start growing quickly without much UX oversight. Companies that have multiple groups working simultaneously on different features are particularly susceptible to this problem, since new sections of the product can be built with little to no knowledge of other features that are also being designed.

The biggest problem with inconsistency is that it's mentally taxing for your users. Imagine if every time you went to a product page on Amazon you had to actively search for the buy button because it was always in a different place. I'll bet you'd buy less stuff. (Note to Amazon: Please move the buy button randomly. I'm going broke here.)

Inconsistency also makes your product feel less finished and professional, which can be a serious problem for companies who are hoping that people will give them money.

An important tool in combating inconsistency is understanding why your product is becoming inconsistent in the first place. If it's because you're shipping things too fast to keep them consistent, then you can solve this problem by doing quick sweeps periodically to find the inconsistencies and fix them.

If, on the other hand, it's being caused because you have too many people working on different features, you can often reduce the problem by using simple style guides and frameworks, which I discuss in the next section.

And, of course, if you're being inconsistent because you just can't be bothered to be consistent...well, cut it out. You're making yourself look bad, and it's really easy to fix.

Frameworks

The best part about building products these days is that, in many cases, somebody else has already done a lot of the boring, repetitive work.

That's certainly true of frameworks. What's a framework? It's one of the many, many free products available to help you design and build your product quickly.

For example, if you're building a web application, using something like Bootstrap or Foundation can provide you with a responsive grid-style interface with decent styling and some common JavaScript tools that are trivially simple to use.

Using a framework means you don't have to spend a huge amount of time creating a custom visual design for your product. Even if you want to do some customization, it still makes designing and prototyping much faster, since things like lightboxes, tooltips, button styles, and dozens of other tools are already built in.

And in case you're worried that your site will end up looking just like every other site out there, they're quite easy to customize. For example, both of these are built on top of Bootstrap. One's been skinned a bit. I'll bet you can tell which one.

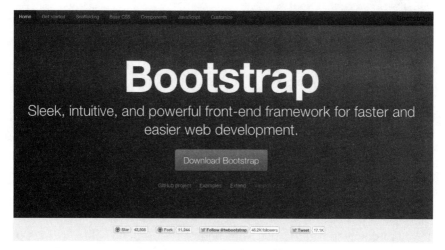

Figure 7-3. The framework

Figure 7-4. The final product

The other lovely thing about these frameworks is that they tend to be responsive, so that you can use the same code for desktops, tablets, and smartphones. This will save you a ton of time and make you look like a genius, since you will have designed for all major platforms at once.

There's Probably a Plug-in for That

Let's say that it is absolutely critically important that you include comments on your product pages. Ask yourself this very important question: "Is there anything particularly innovative or different about my comment system?" No? Great, use the ones somebody else built.

That's right; there are like a billion plug-ins and services that let you easily add all sorts of things to your product until you have time to build it yourself. Vanity or Optimizely let you do A/B testing. Facebook lets you add comments. Badgeville lets you add badges, if that's something that you feel compelled to do (for reasons that escape me). Products like Spree Commerce, Shopify, and Magento let you add an entire storefront.

If you're doing something that somebody else has done before as part of your product, then leverage that. You don't get extra points for building everything from scratch right from the beginning.

Sure you're probably going to want to change it later, but that's what Lean is about. Find out if it's useful to your users, double down on the things they like, and get rid of the things they don't. It really does save you a huge amount of time.

Don't Design It at All

This falls into a similar camp as the plug-ins, but I've had very good luck simply using somebody else's platform and themes entirely for the original version of products.

For example, if you're thinking of building some sort of contest functionality, why not try running it first on Facebook using one of the services that help you run social media promotions? Personally, I've used Offerpop and Wildfire, but new tools appear every day, so make sure to find one that runs the kind of promotion that will work best for your test.

The idea here is that you can validate or invalidate the concept first before you start to measure the changes you can make with new features or a better-designed user experience.

There are lots of different platforms you can use to get your first product out the door with minimal design decisions. If you're not interested in using Facebook, there are hundreds of WordPress plug-ins and templates you can use to get a very simple product up and running.

Remember, the goal for this sort of thing is to validate your hypotheses with the minimum amount of design and coding. You'll almost certainly move quickly to something where you have more control, but you'll do it when you have more information about the right things to design and build.

Getting Some Professional Help

A lot of people compare finding a good UX designer with finding a unicorn. Unicorns are notoriously hard to recruit and surprisingly difficult to work with. I always think a Fabergé egg is a better comparison. I mean, at least those exist, although they are rather expensive and not too easy to find.

Figure 7-5. Only slightly harder to hire than a designer

That said, sometimes it's worth it to get a little bit of professional help for certain parts of your product. You don't get a prize for designing it all yourself, you know.

A key factor in hiring a contract designer is establishing exactly what kind of designer she is. For example, you wouldn't hire me to make your product pretty. I don't make products pretty. I make them easy to use.

Other designers specialize in other areas. Unfortunately, it seems like every designer has made up her own title, and the ones that match don't necessarily do the same things.

To make sure you're talking to the right sort of person, first you need to figure out exactly what you're hiring her for.

Here are a few of the kinds of projects that might be really easily handled by a contract designer:

- You want a better checkout flow.

- Your visual design and branding need a refresh with no feature changes.

- You are thinking of adding a new feature, and you want to make sure you're building what users really need.

- You need a brochure site built for your physical product.

These are all wildly different types of projects, and you'd potentially need different types of designers to create them. For example, a checkout flow requires a well-thought-out information architecture, a working knowledge of how to keep people from abandoning shopping carts, and a strong grounding in basic usability techniques. A new visual design refresh, on the other hand, requires outstanding style and understanding of how colors, layout, and typography can be used effectively, and the ability to redesign a page without making it harder to use.

Interestingly, despite the near-universal demand for designer portfolios, I'd say that it's virtually impossible to judge a person's ability to do any of the above tasks by looking at a static page of her work.

Here's a better way to pick the right kind of contract designer for you. Explain exactly what you think the problem you want to solve is. Make sure that you include things like success criteria and how you will measure it. Then ask her to show you something from her body of work that she think is somehow similar. It doesn't have to be in the same space. It just has to show similar types of thought processes.

Have the designer walk you through what exactly she did on the project, and why she made the choices she made. Even if you don't particularly like the final outcome, this interview process will help you to understand how the designer thinks about design and how she might approach your project.

So, if you're looking for somebody to create a great checkout flow, and every decision she makes is based on what looks the prettiest, she's probably not the right designer for you. On the other hand, if you're looking for a fabulously stylish visual redesign of a flow that's already been optimized for simplicity and funnel conversion, you'll probably want somebody with a great visual style rather than somebody who is entirely concerned with usability.

Loosely Related Rant: The Art of the UX Steal

I've been building interfaces for a very long time, and I can tell you that the number of times I've had to solve a completely new and unusual user problem is remarkably small. This isn't surprising. The vast majority of products we build incorporate a lot of familiar elements.

For example, think about the number of products you use that include one or more of the following: login, purchasing, comments, rating systems, order history, inventory management, or user-generated content.

Do you expect that every single login experience gets redesigned completely from scratch in a vacuum? Of course not! It would be annoying if they were, since each new version would almost certainly differ just enough to make things confusing. Having design standards for things like logging in makes a lot of sense for both users and designers.

However, this tendency to fall back on patterns, or just to copy whatever Apple/Amazon/ Facebook is doing, can cause some problems, especially for startups. There are a few big reasons why you shouldn't just adopt another company's solution without serious consideration.

They May Not Want Exactly What You Want

Companies have hidden agendas. But their agenda is not always your agenda, which means that their optimal design is not your optimal design. And if you think that they're always optimizing for the best user experience, you've lost your damn mind.

Want an example? OK! Have you ever purchased an item and been opted in to receiving email deals from the company's partner sites? As a user, who likes that? Who thinks that's a great user experience? Exactly.

Then why do companies do it? They do it because they have made the business (not UX) decision that they make more money by opting people into partner deals than they lose by slightly annoying their customers. That's a totally reasonable calculation for them to do.

Now let's say your biz dev person comes to you and says he wants to add that feature to your checkout process because he has a partner lined up who is willing to pay for the privilege of getting your users' email addresses. He says it will be OK to add the feature because other big companies are doing it, so it must make money.

But you have no idea how much money they're getting for making their UX worse. You have no idea of the number of users they may be losing with this practice. And even if you did know their numbers, you can't decide whether this feature is the right business decision for you until you know what those numbers are going to be for your product.

In an ideal world we could always just choose whatever made the best possible user experience, but realistically, we make these kinds of business/ UX trade-offs all the time. They're inevitable. Just make sure that you're making them based on realistic estimates for your product and not on the theory that it's right because a bigger company is doing it.

They Don't Do Exactly What You Do

By my count, Amazon has sold at least one of pretty much everything in the world. OK, I'm just extrapolating from my purchase habits, but you know what I mean.

Not only does it sell products directly, but it also allows other companies and individuals to sell through its marketplace. It also sells a lot of different versions of the same product. This makes its product pages pretty complicated.

Does your product do all of those things? If you work for a startup, I certainly hope not, since many of Amazon's features were added over the course of more than a decade.

If your product doesn't have all those features, then you might want to do all sorts of things differently than Amazon does. For example, your product pages could be significantly simpler, right? They could emphasize entirely different things, or have a clearer call-to-action, or more social proof because they don't need to account for all of Amazon's different features.

Whether or not you even have product pages, the point is that no other company is doing exactly what you're doing (or if it is, you have an entirely different problem), so its optimal UX is, by necessity, going to be different from yours.

They Can Get Away with It

If Dante were writing today, the ninth circle of Hell would have involved trying to sign in to multiple Google accounts at once. True story.

A friend of mine decided to make me angry the other day, so he showed me a Google Docs screen where the Save button was so cleverly hidden it took him several minutes to locate it. This was on a screen that had maybe four elements, and he's a very senior software engineer, so this probably wasn't user error. I find the usability on certain Google products almost sadistically poor, although I will give them credit for frequently iterating and fixing many of the things I initially find hard to use.

I put up with what is sometimes a suboptimal user experience because Google provides me with incredible value for free that I can't get anywhere else even by paying for it.

I don't use things like Google Docs for their UX. In fact, I use them in spite of large portions of their UX. And if your UX borrows from Google through some misguided notion that just because Google does it, it must be right, I will quit your product in a freaking heartbeat and bad-mouth it to all my friends.

The moral of this story isn't just "don't steal UX from Google," although that's not bad advice. The moral is that very few companies succeed in spite of their UX, and if you happen to steal UX from them, you're doing it wrong.

On a side note, you know what has a fabulous UX? The original Google product—the one where there was just a single search box, two buttons, and a hugely successful algorithm for finding great results. Unsurprisingly, that's the UX that got us all hooked in the first place.

The Right Way to Steal

Now that the horror stories are out of the way, you still shouldn't be coming up with every design element from scratch.

Not only is it OK to steal a basic login process from another product (although not Google), it's almost certainly the best possible thing you could do. Having a nonstandard way for users to log into your product is just needlessly confusing.

One product I use on a regular basis used to have its Log In button on the top left of the home page instead of the top right. This little change meant that several times I had a hard time remembering how to get into the product and wasted several seconds searching for the button. I probably wasn't the only one to complain, since they fixed it relatively quickly.

Logging in isn't the only thing to standardize. Anytime you have a simple activity that users do regularly in lots of other products, you should at least check to see whether there is a standard and consider adopting it.

Of course, you can always choose not to do things the way everybody else is doing them, but you should have a very strong reason for changing things, and you should definitely A/B test your change against the standard design pattern.

Trust but Verify

Most importantly, when you are planning on stealing—or "adopting a standard" as we're now going to euphemistically call it—it's still important to test it.

As I mentioned before, I like to do quick qualitative tests to observe some people using the standard. In fact, often I'll test the standard on competitors' products before implementing it, rather than implementing it and then finding out that it's bad. Then I'll test again once it's implemented in my product.

In general, the more companies who are doing things identically the less likely it is to be confusing. But it's still necessary to make sure that the design works in the context of the rest of your product.

Go Do This Now!

- Learn from others: Try checking out sites like PatternTap (*http:// patterntap.com/*) or Mobile Patterns (*http://www.mobile-patterns. com/*) to see examples of common design elements.

- Learn from your competitors' mistakes: Try running a usability test on a competitor's product in order to see where it's failing so you won't make the same mistakes it does.

- Check for consistency: Try visiting every screen or state of your product or site to see how consistent you're really being about things like navigation, header elements, vocabulary, and visuals.

CHAPTER 8

Diagrams, Sketches, Wireframes, and Prototypes

In this chapter:

- Learn the difference between a wireframe, a sketch, and an interactive prototype.

- Understand when you can save time by skipping higher fidelity design deliverables.

- See the drawbacks of paper prototyping.

Up to now, I've talked rather vaguely about "design," but UX design isn't synonymous with creating big, pixel-perfect Photoshop files. In fact, in many ways, starting a design in Photoshop is the opposite of Lean.

As we've already explored, starting a design means starting with a hypothesis and designing tests to validate or invalidate that hypothesis. The Photoshop mockup of a final screen is a very tiny part of the entire user experience, and in many cases it should be skipped entirely. The UX is what the user is going to do and how she is going to do it, as well as what the product is going to look like.

But, still, we need to create something. It can't all be scribbles on whiteboards and enthusiastic hand waving.

At some point, we need to create designs. For the purpose of this chapter, a "design" is going to be represented by some artifact that fulfills one of several very different types of functions.

113

These artifacts might be one of the following:

- A diagram
- A sketch
- A set of wireframes
- An interactive prototype
- A visual design

They are all at very different levels of fidelity, and they're all used for very different functions in design.

The most important thing to remember is that, to create a good design, you don't need to do all of these. In fact, often you'll want to produce only one or two different artifacts for any particular thing you're designing. The trick is knowing which one you want to produce at any given time.

In this chapter, I'm going to give you a high-level overview of what each of these design deliverables is, why you might make it, and when you should skip it. As with the other design chapters, I want you to understand that you shouldn't necessarily be creating all of these things for every design change. Sometimes you'll want one of these artifacts, while other times you may need several.

Remember, design is about creating an experience, and these are tools that can help you create and communicate that experience. No single tool is important on its own. All of these tools can help you flesh out your designs and explain your ideas to your coworkers or users. They're all helpful at different points in the process.

Confused? Yeah, I get that. Let's look at some examples.

Why Diagram?

There are all kinds of different diagrams, but the ones I'm referring to here are the kind that help you figure out the flow of a complex interaction.

Now, when I say "complex interaction" you may think to yourself, "Oh, I'm good, then. Everything on my site is really simple!" You would be wrong.

Let's take a "simple" interaction like signing into a product. Seems pretty straightforward, right? You get a username or email address and maybe a password, and you're good to go.

Figure 8-1. Something that seems simple...

Except, what if the user enters the wrong password or you can't find the email address in your database? You should probably have an error state for that, maybe even two different error states, depending on how you want to treat this error.

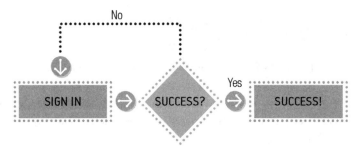

Figure 8-2. ...can become complicated

Or what if the user has forgotten her password? You should probably have some way for her to recover it. There are a few different options, but you'll need to figure out which one is right for you.

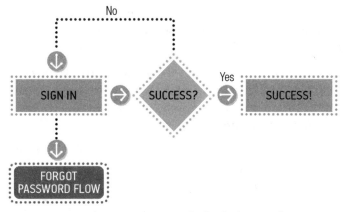

Figure 8-3. You can even find whole new flows

Oh, how about if the user hasn't actually created an account yet? You'll need to let her create one here.

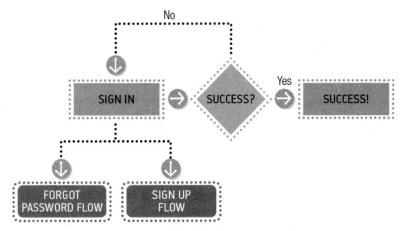

Figure 8-4. I could go on, but you get the point

And don't even get me started if you also want to offer different ways to sign in, like Twitter or Facebook, or allow people to sign into multiple accounts. That just gets crazy.

My point is that any interaction that is more than one or two steps or that has the potential for branching or errors can often be helped by a simple flow diagram.

The diagrams aren't merely exercises in documentation. They're a way for you to visualize your design and decide which states need designs. For example, does this particular flow need some sort of error state? Does it need synchronous interactions like responding to an email? Does it need to respond in different ways to user input?

Once you start to think through all the different possible flows, you get a much clearer view of the amount of design and engineering you need to do, which in turn will help make it easier to predict the amount of work that needs to go into your feature.

If you're working on an application that is a series of screens, like a web application or a mobile app, you may also want to do some sort of site map or navigational diagram.

While site maps may seem less useful now that everything is an application, you'll find that many products have some sort of navigational flow that can be expressed in a site map.

For example, imagine a shopping application. There's a lot of information architecture involved in allowing people to quickly find a product in a catalog.

If you want your users to never get lost while using your product, you'd better start by making sure that you know where everything should go.

What's It Good For?

Use a flow diagram or a site map when you're trying to figure out how users will move around your product and complete common tasks. It can also be extremely helpful for estimating how much time something will take to build and for communicating the design to engineers.

It's not particularly good for validating a hypothesis or for testing for usability, since these are not artifacts that are meant to be shown to users. Don't worry. We'll get to some methods that will help with that.

How Can You Make One?

As I just mentioned, these are not meant to be shown to users, so any time you spend making these pretty or interesting is just a total waste of time. These are items that are meant for purely internal consumption, so make them incredibly clear and easy to understand, but don't bother with the bells, whistles, and gradients.

My favorite tools for making diagrams like this are Visio or OmniGraffle. I've also made them in Balsamiq, on whiteboards, and on Post-It notes. Really, you should just use whatever you're comfortable with.

One technique that can be kind of fun is to create sketches of expected screens and print them out onto pieces of paper, which you then move around physically.

The most important thing to remember about diagrams is that they will change. Sometimes a lot. Don't feel like, just because you've made a flow diagram, you've got everything figured out. I can't tell you the number of times that I've made a lovely flow for a particular task—for example, checking out with an online cart—and then found a whole new path that I needed to add later, as soon as I began prototyping.

Because they change, I strongly recommend using some sort of tool that allows you to easily update the diagram, since an out-of-date diagram is just wildly confusing.

When Do You Sketch?

There is an important concept in design that you've probably never noticed, but that has affected absolutely every interface you've ever used. Some things need to be close to other things.

There's a technical term for this, but I'm not telling you what it is, because it's not particularly important. Well, the term isn't important. The concept is critical.

Figure 8-5. One of these makes it easier to buy than the other

My friend Jenny, an interaction designer, tells the story of the time she asked her husband to put up a sign asking people not to ring the doorbell, because the baby was sleeping. A little while later, someone came to the door and rang the doorbell.

After she answered the door, she realized the problem. Her husband had put the sign on the door.

Now, that placement makes some intuitive sense. A person comes to the door. They see the sign. They read it. They don't ring the doorbell.

But there was a much better placement for the sign. Jenny moved the sign to hang directly over the doorbell. Nobody rang it again.

Why am I telling you this story? You're not designing doorbells. I'm telling you because it illustrates how important the placement of information is. Critical information must be placed in very close proximity to whatever call-to-action it concerns. In other words, you need to put the sign in a place where people are forced to read it as they are in the act of starting to ring the doorbell.

By the same logic, you need to put the buy button very close to the price of an item, because that is critical information that the user needs at the moment of decision. You must put error messages where the error that needs to be fixed has occurred.

Please
Knock!
Baby is
sleeping!

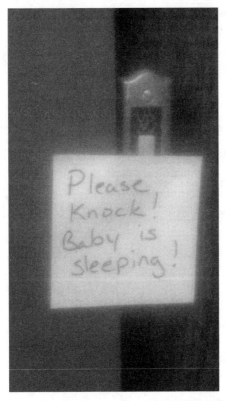

Figure 8-6. Hard to miss when it's in the right place

Figure out which part of the form is not filled in correctly.

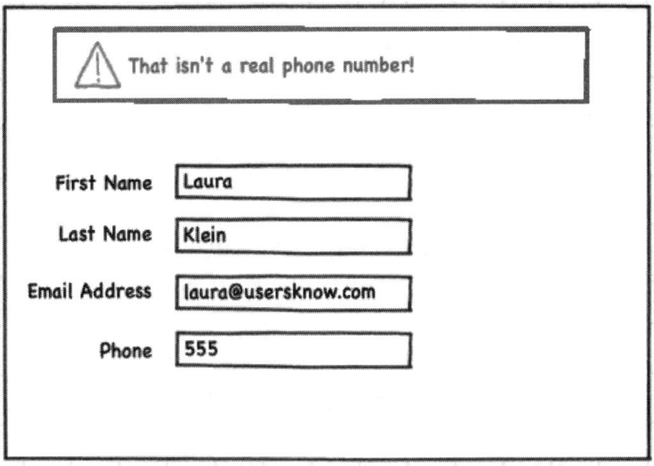
That isn't a real phone number!
First Name
Laura
Last Name
Klein
Email Address
laura@usersknow.com
Phone
555

Figure 8-7. The user has to read the error message here

Error messages are often put at the top of forms. Unsurprisingly, they're often missed by users, who have to spend time figuring out what they did wrong.

OK, how about this one?

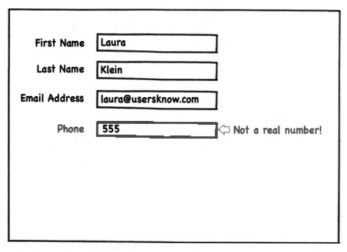

Figure 8-8. Inline errors make it easier to discover the problem

Doesn't that make it clearer?

You need to do this with every piece of critical information and call-to-action on your product. Once you start thinking of design this way, you will be shocked at how few applications get this right.

And this is where sketching comes in.

What's It Good For?

As with diagrams, sketching is incredibly useful for helping you to think through problems.

Sketching is the first time that you start to visualize your product or feature. You stop thinking of it as "User needs to log in" and start thinking of it as a group of elements that a user would need to log in. You also start to think of where those elements go in relation to one another.

You do it in a sketch because sketches are quick and disposable. You can throw a bunch of elements onto a page and move them around and toss some and add some new ones in a matter of minutes. You can make a half-dozen sketches, each of which presents different elements, or groups information differently. You can experiment easily.

Sketching can also be great for starting to communicate your design to other people. If you've got a good enough engineering team and a simple enough feature, a quick sketch can be all that's needed to get a version of a feature built.

If it's not such a simple feature, then combining a series of sketches with a flow diagram to show how they all fit together can be a good way to go.

Sketches are less good for getting feedback from users, unfortunately. While you can get some overall information from them by showing a sketch, too often you're simply asking them to fill in information on their own. People who are unfamiliar with your product are not going to be able to form much of an opinion when faced with a static sketch.

How Can You Make One?

My absolute favorite tool for this is Balsamiq, but there are lots of good, easy-to-use ones out there, including things like Mockingbird, MockFlow, OmniGraffle, and paper templates for various different mediums. There are dozens of others you can use at all price points and levels of complexity. Find the kind that works for you.

Lots of people go for pencil and paper, and that's fine, but it has some drawbacks. It's hard to keep paper sketches up to date or to change them much. After you've moved a few things around, they can tend to look like nothing more than a bunch of scribbles.

Also, they're hard to keep around for reference later. I have thousands of sketches of various projects stored on my computer, and I can generally find the one I'm looking for. I couldn't have nearly that many in hard copies.

Once you have your tool, just start putting things together. Group them loosely. Think about the hierarchy of your screen, or, if you're not designing for a screen, the context in which you'd like to present things.

Put simply, figure out what goes with what. If you show user information, do you also want to show a picture? A name? Other identifying information? If you're showing a list of things, what things would a user need to know about each item to select from that list? Is it a single list or is the list split into smaller lists for quicker skimming? Does everything fit in one place, or do you need to split things up so that you don't have information overload in one area? Should things be done in steps?

The only way to learn to sketch better is to sketch. A lot. Go create a sketch. Then do it again.

What's a Wireframe, and Why Do You Care?

It turns out that there's no definitive consensus as to what exactly a wireframe is. I know. I was annoyed as you are when I found out.

I've seen wireframes so high level that they look like they're just a series of boxes. I've also seen them so detailed that they are practically at the point of an interactive prototype. What someone defines as a wireframe appears to depend entirely on who taught him to design.

But the important thing about wireframes is what they are used for. A wireframe, for me, is somewhere between a rough sketch and an interactive prototype. It's when I really start thinking about a feature's details at the screen level.

A useful wireframe, in my opinion, needs to include all the copy, buttons, calls-to-action, and navigation elements of a real product. It doesn't have any visual design yet. That comes later. But it's definitely where you're taking all the elements that you sketched out and making sure that they not only fit together on one screen but that they also hold up throughout an entire feature or product.

For example, if you're creating a feature to allow people to post pictures of their children, your wireframe is where you're going to figure out all the privacy settings and the upload settings and the filtering and sorting. All of them. You don't just scribble in a little drop-down menu with the words, "some sort of filter" like you might in a sketch. You specify whether people want to see photos of only their children or if they want to see pictures of other people's children, and how they would do that.

It's where you decide how much content you need in order to describe the feature and where it should go contextually on the screen. I once saw someone try to pass something off as a wireframe that had nothing but lorem ipsum text on it. Nothing at all. I laughed at them and told them that what they had shown me was a series of rectangles.

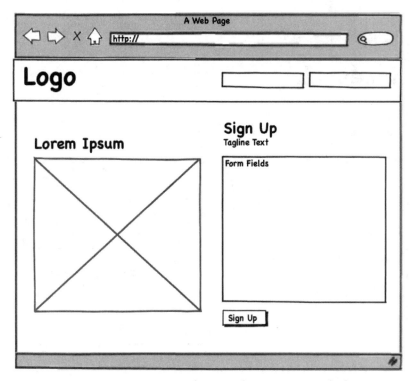

Figure 8-9. Not a wireframe. Also, not particularly helpful.

Content is critical to wireframes, because without it, you don't actually know how much space to leave for it. This is where you're figuring out if everything you want really does fit together on a screen, and you can't do that if you don't know whether you're going to need a line of text or a novel.

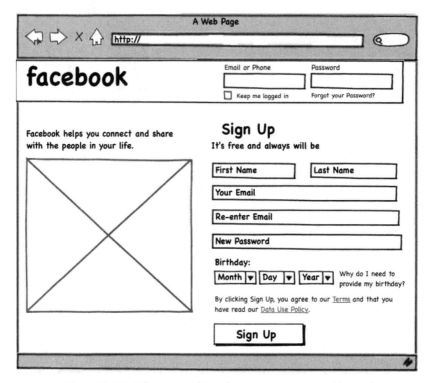

Figure 8-10. The same thing but now recognizable and more useful

While you can make wireframes at all sorts of different levels of fidelity, the most important thing is to remember that this is where you're figuring out everything that goes into each screen or mode of your product.

If you can hook multiple wireframes together, you can even create a very simple version of an interactive prototype, which can be wildly useful, since it gives you 80% of the benefits of a fully interactive prototype with far less work.

What's It Good For?

Wireframes are awesome because they are good for so many things. I use wireframes for figuring out this deeper level of design. By forcing myself to write copy, I come to understand what a screen is really about. By forcing myself to fill in a filter drop-down box, I'm thinking through many different user stories and trying to anticipate what a person might think or feel when interacting with the screen.

But they're not just good for the designer. Wireframes, especially when you string a few together, are high enough fidelity to start to get good usability feedback on them. They look enough like a real product that users can react to them and tell you things like what they think a screen does or how they would accomplish a task by using them.

They're also pretty much my go-to replacement for design specs. Back in the day, we used to write multipage documents specifying every single different thing a product would do and every different error state a user might encounter. It was like a horrible, complicated essay paper that engineers hated to read as much as we hated to write. It was a dark time.

Then I realized that, instead of giving people a giant written document, I could just show them exactly what was supposed to be on a screen. It could include all the different states right there. Want to know what's in a drop-down list? Click on it! Want to know where the error messages go and what they say? They're all right there in context.

A single wireframe is worth a hundred stories in Pivotal Tracker and a dozen pages of unread design spec. I'm not overselling this. If you learn how to do one thing, learn how to make a very detailed wireframe.

How Can You Make One?

This is tricky. Much as there are a hundred different definitions of what a wireframe is, there are as many different products that promise to help you make them. I'm sure they're all great. I haven't used the vast majority of them, because I've got stuff that works for me.

For low-fidelity wireframes that are a step above a sketch, I tend to use Balsamiq. For higher fidelity wireframes that have a little more interactivity, I use HTML and CSS. This means I can easily convert the higher fidelity ones to an interactive prototype.

But you can make them however you want. Some of the nice programs that people use to create wireframes are Axure, OmniGraffle, Mockingbird, JustInMind, and dozens of others. Seriously, Google it. There have probably been six more wireframing tools created in the time it took for you to read this.

Do You Have to Make an Interactive Prototype?

You never have to make a fully interactive prototype. Except for when you do. Because sometimes it's really the only way that you're going to avoid a huge amount of rework later.

There are only a few reasons for making an interactive prototype, and one of them is stupid.

The stupid reason for making one is that you are going to use it to sell an idea to an investor or somebody higher up in your organization. If you're doing this, you should consider quitting. Honestly, if anybody thinks a full interactive prototype is a reason to give you money, they should learn about things like traction.

The best reason for making an interactive prototype is to figure out all the things that are wrong with your design before you spend a lot of time and money building your real product. You see, the only thing better for usability testing than an actual product is a close facsimile of that actual product.

So here's the deal. If you have a very complicated product or feature that would take a very long time to build, or if you have a product that, for some reason, you won't be able to easily and quickly fix, it is worth making an interactive prototype. If you have a question about two very different approaches to an interactive feature, you might want to prototype both of them and test them against each other.

Basically, you use interactive prototypes when they will save you time and money by allowing you to test something that is very close to a real product without having to bother to build the whole thing.

Here's an example. I was working with a client that made a product for small businesses. The product really worked best once the users connected it to all their financial accounts, kind of like Mint.

The client wanted a simpler way to get people connected to their accounts. The problem, as is often the case with outside integrations, was that making changes to the way this worked was big and complicated and hard.

Now, that by itself isn't too much of a problem. Engineers tackle big, complicated, hard problems all the time. The problem was that, based on user research, we had a few different approaches to the problem, and we weren't entirely sure which would be the best method.

This is pretty typical. You can understand a user's problem perfectly but still have a few different ideas of how to solve the problem.

Now, in a world with unlimited resources, we could have just built all three different approaches and put them into production and watched to see how they performed. In fact, if the differences had been small, like messaging or button placement, this is almost certainly what we would have done.

But the differences weren't small. That's why we built interactive prototypes.

Once we had three different interactive prototypes, which were built in a fraction of the time it would eventually take to build the real feature, we were able to do some basic usability testing.

We ran five people through each of the three prototypes and asked them to perform the main task—connecting their financial accounts. There was no backend to the system, so the interactions were all entirely fake, but they felt real enough for users to understand what was going on and to react in the same way they would normally.

Obviously, we followed all the best practices for testing—not leading the users, mixing up the order in which they tried the different prototypes, getting a decent mix of user types, etc.

At the end of the test, all five of the users were able to complete the tasks easily with one of the prototypes. With another, they were able to complete the tasks, but they were slower and had more questions during the process. With the final prototype, which had been built to imitate the behavior of the feature that was already in production, a few of the users weren't even able to complete the tasks.

We also found a few problems and questions that came up during the prototype testing that we were able to fix before the feature was built, which meant less work after we launched the feature.

What's It Good For?

So the important thing about interactive prototypes is that they're great for testing your product with real users when building different variations of a feature would simply take too long in production or be extremely hard to fix later.

Anytime you're creating something that you can't easily fix after you've released it, like a physical device or boxed software, interactive prototypes are crucial for finding as many problems as possible before your product is in the hands of users.

Similarly, if you're building something you need to get right the first time or that will be used only once, it is incredibly important to test the product or feature in a state that is as close as possible to the real thing.

How Can You Make One?

This is entirely dependent on what you're building. For web applications, the best interactive prototyping tool is HTML, CSS, and JavaScript. This may be the best interactive prototyping tool for mobile apps, as well, since it allows you to quickly build, test, and iterate on your design.

However, if you are a masochist and love Flash or Silverlight or some other sort of impossible tool, feel free to use one of those. If you're a programmer, go ahead and build the prototype in whatever language you're comfortable with. The trick is to acknowledge that this is a disposable item, so you should build it in a way that isn't going to break your heart when you toss it all and build it from scratch the right way.

So Which Should You Build?

The key is to remember that, the closer you get to reality, the better information you'll get. It's also important that you not build more than you need to get the sort of information you want.

For example, it's stupid to spend time building a full-scale interactive prototype with a complete visual design in order to get some feedback on messaging. You can test your messaging with a landing-page test or a quick A/B test.

On the other hand, trying to test a complicated interactive feature with a rough sketch is simply not going to get you the kind of information you need.

Also, consider the needs of the engineering team building the feature. How much guidance do they need? Do they need every single interaction fully scoped out? Sometimes they do. Other teams working on other features can be given a wider scope for interpretation of the design.

If you trust your engineering team to make some interaction design decisions, then you can present them with lower fidelity mocks and work through things like corner cases with them as they build. I often do this sort of thing with my team, and I find it saves us all a lot of time. Then again, I work with incredibly brilliant senior engineers, which, obviously, I recommend as another best practice.

Whatever happens, do not feel like you need to go through every one of these steps with every feature or product you build. I would say that I rarely go through more than one or two of these when I'm adding features to an existing product.

Let's face it, most features you're adding to an existing product aren't huge. A lot of work we do as designers involves testing minor iterations. Spending time doing diagrams, sketches, wireframes, and prototypes can be a giant waste of time if you're adding comments to a product page.

However, it is critical that you make a conscious decision every time about whether you are going to go through a particular step. Don't decide not to prototype because you don't have time. Decide not to prototype because your particular feature really doesn't need it or because there's a faster way to get the information you need. Decide not to diagram because the feature isn't complicated enough to warrant it, not because you don't know how.

Make sure that you fully understand the benefits and drawbacks of each step and make the decision about whether or not to use it every single time. It will quickly become second nature to you, but until it does, you need to go through the process.

Should You Make It Pretty?

Premature prettification is the cause of more UX disasters than Myspace. There, I said it.

Whether you are at the diagramming, sketching, wireframing, or prototyping step, the one thing you should not be concentrating on is making it gorgeous.

Yes, make it clean. Make it clear. Make it obvious. Do not obsess over fonts or gradients or colors. Definitely include some images. Do not spend any time making sure those images are perfect or well lit or even decently cropped.

Spending time making things pretty at this stage is just a colossal waste of time, largely because you're going to have to change bunches of it after you run your user tests and figure out all the stuff you screwed up. You don't want to know how awful it is to spend days putting every pixel in its right place and then throw it all out and start over when it turns out your navigation structure was dead wrong.

Also, getting everything pixel perfect is going to make you far less likely to want to make sweeping changes to your design, even if it's necessary. The mere fact that you spent hours of your time or thousands of your dollars getting a design to look fabulous is going to get in your way if you have to, for example, throw out the entire main page because it confused people.

The other, less obvious, problem with making gorgeous prototypes, is that user-test subjects are less likely to give you critical feedback on usability. A strong visual design can be very distracting, and test participants will tend to focus on the visual aspects of the design, no matter how many times you tell them they shouldn't.

Also, a fully visually designed prototype feels more "done." There is a tendency by user testers to be polite, and the more finished a product feels, the more likely they are to not want to give you any bad feedback about it.

I'm not saying you won't get any useful feedback. I'm just saying that you'll get better, more usability-focused feedback if you eliminate visual design during the testing phase.

The last reason you shouldn't make things pretty at this stage is because you will subconsciously start making compromises to suit the visual design before you've fully thought out the user experience. When you start spending time focusing on things like what the buttons are going to look like, you narrow your vision and stop thinking about the bigger issues, like whether you have the right buttons at all.

This is a serious problem. This early part of the design process is when you figure out the big problems, like navigation and grouping of features and what tasks and flows a user will encounter. It's very hard to think about all those things while simultaneously finding the perfect shade of blue.

It's not that the perfect shade of blue isn't important. It can be tremendously important. It's just important later in the process. After all, you might end up getting rid of all the elements of your interface that you were going to make blue once you realize that they're just confusing the hell out of your users.

So, not only am I giving you permission not to spend any time on visual design at this stage, but I'm also telling you that you absolutely must not spend time thinking about visual design at this point, no matter how much you want to.

As a final note of caution, I'll just mention that, if you're working with an outside agency of any sort, it is almost certainly spending time making its deliverables attractive. It is generally not in the best interest of an agency to show work that looks half-finished or ugly. This is a fairly significant problem because you're paying for the hours they spent making a work in progress look great.

My suggestion is to always ask for the agency to share as much of the work product as possible rather than waiting to share pixel-perfect mockups and finished designs. The earlier you can see the design, the more likely you are to be able to fix things that aren't testing well without having to pay an arm and a leg to get everything made pretty more than once.

Loosely Related Rant: Why I Hate Paper Prototypes

Every interaction designer I've ever met has gone on and on about the virtues of paper prototyping for getting quick feedback from users.

"It's so fast!" they squeal. "You can get great feedback just by dashing off a sketch and showing it to users!"

I will admit that I am in violent disagreement with the majority of people in my discipline, but whenever people suggest paper prototyping as a method for getting actual feedback from actual users, I just want to punch them in the face.

Look, paper prototypes and sketches have their place in interaction design. For example, they're great for helping to quickly brainstorm various different approaches to a problem at the beginning of a design process and I've mentioned a lot of them already in this book.

But, in my opinion, they have several serious drawbacks.

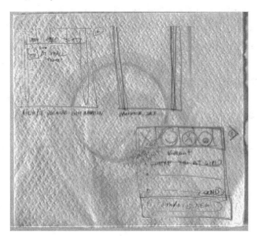

Figure 8-11. Nobody knows what this is

I like sketching in bars as much as the next person, but you have to admit that it's hard to run a decent usability study off of this.

Before I get too far into this, let me define what I mean by a paper prototype, since I've heard people use the term to refer to everything from sketches on actual pieces of paper (or cocktail napkins in a couple of cases) to full-color mockups with a polished visual design.

In this instance, I'm referring to a totally noninteractive screen, mockup, or sketch of any sort of application that is meant to be shared with customers or test participants for the purpose of getting feedback on an idea. It can be printed on actual paper or shown on a computer screen, but whatever the viewer does to it, a paper prototype is not interactive.

So what don't I like about them?

Screen versus Paper

This first peeve applies to screens that are actually printed out or drawn directly on paper. With a few exceptions that I've listed below, I've found this approach to be really counterproductive for getting feedback from people unfamiliar with a product or idea.

Whether they're sketched out by hand or printed out on paper, people interact with paper differently than they do with computer screens. They view them at a different angle. They focus on different parts of the layout. They use their hands rather than a mouse and keyboard to interact with them. They have to shuffle through papers to see various states.

When you show somebody a piece of paper, they are in a different mind-set than they would be if you were to sit them down at a computer or hand them a tablet. They simply don't have the context for understanding what you're trying to show them. When I've tried getting feedback from paper, users have spent far too much time trying to understand what the things on the paper represented. For example, a radio button on a screen is an immediately recognizable thing, while a radio button on paper can often look like a little round circle. All that time spent figuring out what they're looking at completely biases the feedback that the user could give you on the actual idea.

Any feedback you get on a printed design will be colored by the fact that people are interacting with it in a fundamentally different way than they would if it were on a computer screen.

Of course, you can get around this by showing the "paper" prototype on a computer screen, right? Yeah, kind of, except for the following issues.

Animations and interactions

I am an interaction designer. A big part of my job is to determine what happens when a user interacts with a product. Sometimes that's obvious. For example, if I click on a link with some text that reads, "Contact Us," I expect to be able to communicate in some way with the people who have created the product.

But is it so obvious? Back in the day when links could only take you to another static web page, sure it was. But now, all sorts of things could happen. I might have different behavior on hover versus on click. I could be given the option to have a live chat with a rep. I might be presented with an inline contact form so that I don't have to leave the page I'm visiting. The contact form could have some information already pre-filled for me based on my present location or account type. There could be animation involved in displaying the contact information. There could be some sort of contact wizard that would change later screens depending on choices the user makes initially.

All these interactions are much harder to convey with paper prototypes than with interactive wireframes. Sure, you can make a different screen showing each stage of the interaction, but with anything more complicated than a few steps, your observers can get lost pretty fast shuffling through papers.

If you aren't showing the various interaction states to users with your paper prototype, then what exactly are you trying to accomplish? Typically, user research of this sort is useful because it helps you understand whether users can understand an interface or accomplish a task. Reducing the interface to paper makes that nearly impossible.

Now, I've run a lot of user tests. I've run them with working products, interactive prototypes, pictures of screens displayed on computers, pure paper prototypes, and physical mockups of products. I've used prototypes built with everything from HTML to Visio to cardboard.

The one constant was that the closer the prototype mimicked the final product interaction, the fewer problems we found once the product was built. And since I recommend iterative testing during development rather than waiting to test until the product is 100% built (you know, just in case your design wasn't entirely perfect the first time around), an interactive wireframe is the best trade-off of speed for functionality because it allows for natural exploration and discovery on the part of the test subject without requiring a fully working product.

Testing exploration

Paper prototypes, because of their complete lack of interactivity, are totally unsuited to allowing users to explore a product. Let's face it, most of us aren't simply designing a single screen in a vacuum or even a collection of standalone pages.

We're designing products. Products allow users to explore and perform multiple tasks. Think about all the different sorts of activities you might want to perform in an email application, for example. You need to read, send, save, find, and get rid of messages, at a minimum. Each of those tasks has its own flow, and it probably has things that can go right or wrong at each step.

Showing a single page to a user allows you to test only the first step in each of those processes. It doesn't let the user explore naturally and find all sorts of issues. What if they want to start writing a message and then stop to go to another one? What if they accidentally get rid of something? There is literally no way to naturally test these interactions by showing people pieces of paper.

OK, there are exceptions

Given these drawbacks, there are a few situations when designs printed on paper can be used effectively to get feedback from users or to communicate with team members:

1. You are at the very, very earliest stage of design, and you're just brainstorming lots of different ideas with team members to make sure everybody is thinking about the product in the same way. In this case, paper can be very fast and effective, but don't expect that you're going to get very deep into the details without moving to a better medium almost immediately. And you're still not going to show it to a potential user—just members of the team.

2. You're designing material that is meant to be printed, like brochures, user manuals, books, etc. In this case, you want to know how people will interact with the printed media.

3. You're designing a mobile interface. Paper prototyping for mobile is more acceptable than paper prototyping for any other sort of nontouch interface. You still don't get any sort of feedback from your gestures, and it's really awkward to try to understand what happens when you touch parts of the interface, but at least you're not asking people to imagine that they're using a mouse and keyboard. You can get away with this for longer on mobile, but try to move quickly to real prototypes.

4. Your product is an interface for some sort of embedded or small-screen device that would be very difficult to replicate in a quick interactive prototype. For example, a heads-up display for a car dashboard might be hard to show interactively in the appropriate context—although you may also want to consider prototyping on things like iPads when you want to go higher fidelity.

5. You have several different visual designs, and you'd like to show them all to users at the same time in order to see which one is the most attention-getting. You'll still need to show the designs onscreen, of course, since colors can vary so much between screen and print, but it can be helpful to lay out several pieces of paper so that the various options can easily be compared.

6. You need to test designs with people in an environment with absolutely no access to a computer whatsoever. You know, maybe your users are Amish, or you are designing in a post-apocalyptic wasteland where the computers are trying to destroy humanity.

If none of these cases apply and you're designing desktop or web applications for standard computers, then learn to prototype. You'll get infinitely better and more detailed feedback from both users and teammates, and you'll get it earlier in the process.

Go Do This Now!

- Pick a sketching tool: Try getting away from scraps of paper and moving toward something that's easier to test.

- Figure out fidelity: Try looking at the features you're currently designing and determining which deliverables you really need.

- Move out of your comfort zone: If you're used to building all your mocks in Photoshop, try sketching a few versions in Balsamiq. If you sketch everything on a cocktail napkin, maybe try drinking a little less. Also, try an interactive prototype.

CHAPTER 9

An MVP Is Both M & V

In this chapter:

- Learn the concept of the Minimum Viable Product (MVP) and how it affects your UX decisions.

- Understand the difference between a minimal product and a bad product.

I'm sure you've heard of Minimum Viable Products. You've probably even heard people arguing over how minimum and how viable an MVP really has to be. In this chapter, we're going to demystify the MVP and help you understand when they're a good idea.

The concept of the Minimum Viable Product is both great and terrible. It is such a lovely idea—distill your product down to only what is absolutely critical, and don't waste time on anything that isn't necessary.

First things first. What is an MVP? The idea behind a Minimum Viable Product is that, instead of taking months and months building a huge product with dozens of features and all sorts of bells and whistles before finally launching a giant thing that nobody wants, maybe it would be a better idea to launch something smaller and start learning earlier.

The idea is not that you're building a tiny, useless product. The idea is also not that you're building a *bad* product. That is never the idea. The idea is that you're starting with a good, small product and then iterating and adding features that people will use.

This would be absolutely brilliant if anybody was ever able to come to some sort of agreement about the exact set of necessary features for an MVP. After all, it often turns out that things you think are necessary aren't even useful. The problem is that you don't figure that out until after you release your products and see which parts people use.

Figure 9-1. Minimum viable cake

Figure 9-2. Not minimum

Figure 9-3. Not viable

Unsurprisingly, trying to shave a product down to its core is really, really freaking hard. It is perhaps the hardest thing that you will have to do.

After all, how can you determine if one feature you've deemed "unnecessary" is the single thing that's going to make people go absolutely nuts about your product? It's so tempting to just keep piling on features that you "know" are necessary before launching, even if you know you're supposed to be launching a Minimum Viable Product.

The sad truth is that most companies run out of time because they spend far too long tinkering with features that nobody wants and not enough time discovering user problems.

MVPs help solve that problem by making you validate each hypothesis quickly before spending a huge amount of time bolting a tremendous number of supporting features onto a product that doesn't solve a problem.

So let's look at a strategy for building incremental MVPs. By starting very small and then iterating, you're able to learn more quickly and avoid overbuilding.

The Landing Page

Remember how we talked about validating an idea with a landing page? We were able to do that because a landing page can be a Minimum Viable Product.

Some people complain that landing pages aren't really MVPs because, while they're certainly minimal, they're neither viable nor a product. I'd argue they're both.

Landing pages are viable because they answer a question. Remember, in Lean, everything should be a hypothesis that you're either validating or not validating. In this case, the hypothesis is that people are going to be interested enough in what you're offering to request more information or even to promise to pay you when you deliver on that offer.

Instead of thinking of it as a product, think of it as the promise of a product. You're describing a product that you think people will want, driving potential customers to it, and then seeing who shows interest in it on the basis of what you're promising.

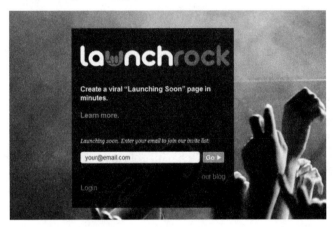

Figure 9-4. Yes, this is an MVP

After all, if people aren't interested enough in your idea to ask for more information, they're almost certainly not going to be interested enough in it to give you their money.

The thing that makes the landing page the best MVP is that you can create a huge number of them for very little investment and with almost no technical knowledge. If you can figure out how to use LaunchRock and Google AdWords, you can create as many MVPs as you like.

You'll learn a huge amount about your product idea as well as your messaging and pricing.

Of course, if you already have a product and are simply looking to add a feature to it, you could think of the landing page as a feature stub instead. Adding a fake buy button to a product page is very similar to creating a landing page for a product that doesn't exist yet. The idea here is to advertise the thing you want to create before you create it and see if there is demand there.

The First Iteration

So once you've launched your landing pages and you're seeing which ideas are getting the best conversion rates, that's when it's time to move into something a little bit bigger.

The important thing here is to stick to what you learned from your last MVP. I can't tell you how often people advertise a very simple concept in their landing page and then go build some enormous behemoth for their first product version.

Look, just because somebody thought your landing page was interesting doesn't mean that they then want to wait 18 months for a fully-fleshed-out version of whatever you were offering. After all, in that amount of time, a dozen competitors could have launched, totally changing the market.

The first iteration of your MVP should focus on delivering exactly the benefit that you were offering in your highest-performing landing-page test.

Here's an example. Imagine that you've run several landing-page tests for some sort of cloud storage system. Now let's say that the best-performing one was focused on sharing sensitive documents securely.

Should your first iteration of the product have a feature that lets people share their documents on Facebook? Probably not. That's got nothing to do with sharing securely, after all. If you've got people who are interested in sharing sensitive documents securely, you should allow them to share sensitive documents securely. And that's pretty much it.

Of course, you're going to have to figure out what it means to your potential customers to share documents securely. You may want to figure out what sorts of documents are most important to them. Do they have special requirements around what "securely" means to them? Do they need to be compliant with some sort of regulations? Do they need some sort of special security?

Luckily, you've collected all those email addresses from people who indicated they were interested in your product, right? Why not set up some calls with them to figure out why they expressed interest in your product? Why not figure out exactly what they imagined they were being promised when they signed up on your very simple landing page.

Once you figure out the single most important feature to the people who showed interest in your very simple offer, you're going to have a pretty good idea for a product that is both minimum and viable.

You're Not Done Yet

It would be lovely if all you ever had to do was create a Minimum Viable Product, but the whole idea is to do that first, and then iterate. So let's talk about how to iterate on it.

After you've got some users trying out your MVP, you're going to get one of several reactions. Ideally, you'll have people who really feel like you're solving a problem for them, and they're super excited about the product, but they'd just like you to add one more little thing...

This is the best of all possible worlds, and your first impulse is going to be to just go ahead and add that one little thing that your customers are begging for. Don't do it. Well, not yet, at least.

What you need at this point is to do some research into how many people are asking for it and why they want it.

Let's say you've created your fabulous, secure-sharing product. Now everybody starts asking for the ability to share things directly on Facebook. You remember, that was the feature you decided not to build because it wasn't part of the MVP.

Your first goal is to go talk to some of the people who are asking for the feature. What you want to ask them is why they want the ability to share on Facebook. You need to figure this out because, depending on their answers, you may in fact build them exactly the feature they're asking for. Alternatively, you may build them the feature they actually need.

Maybe what they actually need is the ability to quickly share their documents with large groups of friends, and they're simply using Facebook as a shorthand for "share this with lots of my friends." But maybe it would actually be a better answer to allow them to import their friends from Facebook into their account and share securely with them that way.

Or maybe they want to share their docs on Facebook. I don't know. Neither do you, and you'll continue not knowing until you ask them.

The point here is that, even if your user base is screaming for a feature, the most important thing you can do is find out why they want that feature so that you can make sure it actually solves their problem.

In the meantime, you can also run some tests to see if it's the sort of feature they might pay you for adding. I'm just throwing that out there.

I said before that your users could have one of several reactions to your initial MVP. Well, another pretty typical one is complete indifference.

Luckily, you didn't build a very large product, and it didn't take very long to build it, so if people are going to be indifferent, now is a great time to find out. Also, the reaction you should have is exactly the same as if people loved your product. You need to reach out to them.

In this case, you're going to want to go back to the folks who initially signed up to hear about your new product from your landing-page tests. In the best-case scenario, you're going to find people who tried your product but who have since stopped using it or who haven't used it much.

You're going to really need to dig. I promise you that at least a few of them will say that they tried it and it was fine, and they're planning on going back and using it any day now. They are lying. You need to figure out what problem they thought your product would solve and why it didn't solve that problem.

Here are some great questions to ask:

- What were you expecting from the product when you signed up?
- What do you feel the product offered?
- How was what the product offered different from what you were expecting?
- How much time did you spend with the product?
- What was your reaction?
- Where did you learn about the product?
- Did you speak with anybody else about the product? If so, who and what did you talk about?

That last question may seem a little odd, but you can learn a lot about who the person thinks your product is for just by asking whom they recommended it to. Also, sometimes people ask friends or coworkers for help, which is good to know, since it may mean that your product was simply too confusing for them to learn on their own.

I know it's tempting to just send an email to all the folks who didn't convert and ask why they stopped using the product. Email is so easy! It takes literally seconds! Some of them will surely write back!

And that's true. A few people will write back and give you a little bit of information about why they aren't using your product. But it's very important that you follow up with them on the phone so you can have a conversation with them. Nobody is going to answer all the above questions in an email, and it's entirely possible that they will tell you things in a conversation that they would never be able to write down.

Frankly, understanding why your MVP isn't working is probably the most important thing you can do. It can literally save your company. Spend some time on it. Reach out personally to people who didn't love your product. Have an honest conversation with them. Thank them for their time. And if you try to get this information by just sending them a survey, I will personally hunt you down and slap you across the face.

One More Time!

OK, it's not just one more time. It's one more time and then another time after that and another after that. In fact, just keep going. Your whole product can be built with small iterations like this.

Observe your users, talk with your users, listen to your users. Then figure out what the next most important thing is to build and build a small version of it. Then improve that until it solves a real problem.

Then do it again.

Meanwhile, use metrics to judge how you're doing. Are people using the new features? Do the new features make you more money? Do they improve retention? Revenue? Referral? Acquisition? Engagement? If not, why not?

One of the most important things about the concept of Minimum Viable Products is that it's not something you do once and then go off and build a giant product. It's an approach to building products and learning from them.

The product itself won't stay minimal for very long, but each feature can be approached like a new MVP.

The steps I've shared are simply one variation of the Minimum Viable Product. You don't have to start with a landing page or a feature stub. You could start with a Wizard of Oz feature or a very small code change. These are the critical parts of the MVP:

- Start small.
- Learn.
- Iterate.

Hopefully that's all starting to sound pretty familiar by now.

Loosely Related Rant: Limited Products versus Crappy Products

One of the reasons that design traditionally takes so damn long is that people try to design more than they need to at once. This is a mistake—sometimes a fatal one.

Well, fatal for your business anyway. You probably won't actually die from overdesign, unless you do something stupid like ask me for help with your terrible, giant, confusing product.

Look, I know that building a product with one or two engineers and no money is tough. As an entrepreneur, you almost certainly have far more ideas than you have resources to create those ideas. And it doesn't help that you have people like me screaming, "Ship it! Ship it!" before you're really ready.

Who could possibly blame you for shipping a product that is, frankly, kind of crappy? I could. Knock it off.

This is the seemingly simple, but often elusive, Minimum Viable Product that you've heard so much about. Too often, people think that the "minimum" part of that gives them license to ship something crappy. What they're doing is totally ignoring the equally important "viable" part of the product.

A crappy product may be minimal, but it sure as hell isn't viable in any real sense of the word. A limited product is both minimal and viable.

Let's take a step back and try to understand the difference between a crappy product and a limited product.

One big difference is that I wholly endorse shipping a limited version of your product. I think it's stupid to ship a crappy product. But what does that mean?

A limited product is something that may not do much, but what it does, it does well. It makes it clear to the user what it does and what he should do. It solves a serious problem, or perhaps a small part of a serious problem. It doesn't crash relentlessly. It doesn't have enormous usability problems. It's not hideous to the point of scaring away your particular market.

It is not half a big product. It is a small but whole product.

Most importantly, a limited product is just big enough and good enough that you can learn something important from it.

But a limited product probably doesn't do anything else. It doesn't have bells and whistles. It doesn't have nice-to-have features. It may solve the problems of only a small subset of the market. It may be released only to beta users.

A crappy product, on the other hand, often tries to do too many things at once, and it doesn't do any of those things particularly well.

You really don't want a crappy product because, when people don't use it, you have no idea if they aren't using it because you have a bad idea or the wrong market, or if it's just because your users are confused and turned off by your crappy product.

Shipping a crappy product is one of the best ways to get a false negative on your idea. People will use products that aren't "polished." They will abandon products that are just bad.

Here's an example: Remember when Amazon sold only books? Back in the '90s, the company that now sells 15 different versions of everything on the planet sold only actual printed books.

And it did it really well. It made it pretty easy to find books. It had a large selection of books. It shipped the books to you reliably. It had nice descriptions of the books. It improved on the bookstore experience by offering me a giant bookstore in my own home.

In other words, it did one thing—sell books online—and it did it well. It wasn't until years later that it even branched out into selling things similar to books. And it wasn't until it was wildly profitable (and no longer a startup) that it started adding advanced features like e-readers, cloud storage, and a marketplace where other people could sell things.

What it didn't do was do a half-assed job of trying to sell you everything immediately. It didn't promise to sell you toasters and jewelry and smoked salmon but then fail to actually ship any of that to your house or charge you three times for the same item. It figured out how to sell things to people online with one understandable market that it could learn from.

Other examples of products that started out doing one thing really well are Instagram, Google Search, and even Facebook. Remember, Facebook started out solving a single problem on a single college campus.

Now, I'm not saying it's easy to build a product to sell books or to share photos or to search the Web. It's not. It's incredibly hard, and it's even harder to get right.

But that's exactly the reason why you need to dramatically limit the scope of your initial product. *Even building something that seems easy is hard to do well.* Imagine how hard it is to build something really big!

So, when I'm yelling at you to Ship It Already, I don't mean that you should ship something bad. I mean that you should ship something limited—something that is small enough to be shippable and usable in a very short amount of time.

And then I mean that you should immediately improve it and ship it again. Do this over and over again as many times as you can for as long as you can.

Eventually, you'll build the product of your dreams. It will probably be quite different from what you originally imagined, but if you want to be an entrepreneur, you're going to have to get used to that.

Go Do This Now!

- Figure out what you want to learn first: Try thinking of a hypothesis you want validated and then come up with an MVP that will help you validate or invalidate that hypothesis.

- Find out how crappy your MVP is: Try contacting some people who have stopped using your product and understand how it failed to live up to their expectations. If all you have is a landing page, then try asking people who have signed up why they signed up and what they're hoping to see.

CHAPTER 10

The Right Amount of Visual Design

In this chapter:

- Learn how much visual design you really need.

- Understand how visual design can affect the usability of your product.

- Learn some tricks for getting a good enough visual design without spending a fortune on an expensive designer.

We've spent a lot of time talking about design, but you'll notice that I haven't really brought up the one thing that most people consider to be "design." In this chapter, we'll finally talk about visual design and how it relates to the user experience of your product.

If one more person confuses visual design and interaction design, I'm going to cry. I can't tell you how many times I've asked people about their UX strategy, and they've said, "Oh, we have someone who knows Photoshop."

Let's go over this one more time for the folks who are still confused: Interaction design and visual design are not interchangeable. Visual design is how something looks. Interaction design is how something works.

Visual design is a part of general user experience design, but user experience design doesn't necessarily have anything to do with visual design.

Let's look at a few examples:

- The exact copy that is shown on a button is a UX question.

- The color of a button and whether it has a gradient is a visual design question.

- How many steps a checkout flow has and which pieces of the flow go on which pages are UX questions.

- The font sizes and colors on the form labels are visual design questions.

As you can imagine, the color of a button can have a large impact on user behavior. However, you shouldn't start a user experience design with the color of a button, because that's leaving out all sorts of important elements of usability, like whether the button should exist in the first place.

In other words, visual design can be a critical part of the user experience, and you shouldn't neglect it. You just shouldn't do it first. Remember, form follows function for a reason. So let's explore how you can get a great visual design in a Lean way.

Why Is Visual Design Important in UX?

I was at a conference recently, and one person asked how important visual design is in user experience, while another asked how much time I spend on visual design early in the design process. The answers to those two questions are "Incredibly important" and "Not much."

A lot of people, even a lot of designers, write off visual design as "making something pretty." Frankly, I've been guilty of this myself. Meanwhile, companies like Google and Facebook have made fortunes while keeping their visual design so spare as to be almost nonexistent.

So you may reasonably wonder, why is visual design important to your startup or new product, and why should you bother spending time and resources on it?

But visual design doesn't just make things pretty. It's instrumental in a lot of ways, including the following:

- Enhancing your information design

- Reinforcing desired user actions

- Setting the tone for your product

Visuals Enhance Information Design

Facebook has a very simple blue, gray, and white look. That's because Facebook is all about delivering an enormous amount of content and information to you quickly. A bright, distracting, or cluttered interface would make it hard to read large numbers of news items and could clash with the very important user-posted pictures.

Figure 10-1. Which is easier to see?

Same with Google. Google, at least the main search product, is about getting you to type in a search term and then giving you access to everything on the Internet that matches it. That's a lot of information to process. Sites that are about delivering large quantities of information need to keep their visual design simple. But a simple design doesn't mean no visual design at all.

Reinforcing Desired User Actions

There is something that you want your users to do with your product. Maybe you want them to buy books or make new friends or search for information. Whatever it is, good visual design can reinforce that behavior by drawing attention to the appropriate parts of the screens.

Consider call-to-action buttons. Something as simple as making them look clickable and noticeable can have a huge impact on whether users follow through on the desired action. This is one of those gray areas where visual design and interaction design converge. A bad visual design can hide important screen elements, rendering a perfectly decent interaction much harder to notice and perform. Conversely, a good visual design can improve the interaction by making important things seem more important.

Figure 10-2. Which of these looks clickable?

Take a look at some of your favorite fashion- or food-related sites. Notice how the visual design tends to favor large images of beautiful products or meals while the rest of the design is kept relatively simple? That's a conscious visual design choice—one that draws attention to the most important parts of the product.

Visuals Set the Tone

One company I worked with had a very distinctive visual design. It featured cartoony characters with giant heads and oversized anime eyes. The colors were bright and cheerful. When we ran usability tests with new people, their first response to the question, "Who is this site for?" was "Pre-teens." Many responded, "Oh, my 12-year-old cousin would love this." It was very clear that these users did not think that the product was for them.

Unfortunately, the product *was* for them. Adults were far more likely than children to spend money on the product, but too many people in that age range felt that the product was for children based on their first impressions of the site and would leave immediately rather than diving in and starting to use it. Luckily, the solution to this was simple. A sophisticated makeover of the visual design, especially concentrating on the landing pages, registration, and first few minutes of use, dramatically improved the response of adult users and increased the percentage who started using the product.

Depending on your industry and market, your company may be trying to convey trustworthiness, edginess, playfulness, warmth, or hundreds of other emotions to your users. Would you put your money in a bank that looked like a surf shop or a fast-food restaurant? You probably wouldn't even go inside. When a user first comes to your site or opens your product, he's making an almost instantaneous decision about whether this product is what he's looking for. Visual design plays a huge role in that decision-making process.

Why I Put Off Visual Design

Just because it's incredibly important doesn't mean that I spend huge amounts of time on visual design early in the process. In fact, I tend to nail down the vast majority of the interaction design before moving on to applying a good visual design. I do this for several reasons:

- It is much faster for me to iterate on something if I don't have to worry about making it pixel perfect. When I get feedback from a user test or a beta customer, simple grayscale wireframes can be changed quickly and without too much regard for things like margins and font sizes, while fully designed visual mockups can take much longer to fix.

- Remember how I said that visual design sets the tone almost instantly for a user? Because of this, visual design can screw up interaction testing. If your tester has an immediate positive or negative reaction to the visuals, you're going to get different information than you would if she could effectively ignore the visuals. Grayscale wireframes or

Balsamiq-style sketches make it much easier to ignore the look and concentrate on the interactions.

- I am going to want to make several versions of visual design to test independently. That's easier for a visual designer to do if he has a reasonably nailed-down version of the wireframes to work from. The last thing you want is to try to test various different versions of visual design along with different versions of interaction design, since it makes it much tougher to know which element is affecting the test results.

- Once some of the basic interactions are scoped, engineering can get to work on the product and then apply a visual design later. This means they're not waiting around for me to get both the interactions and the visual design done up front. Engineering, interaction design, and visual design can all be happening in parallel (provided you have at least three different people to work on the different areas).

- And, of course, if it's a brand-new product, your visual design is going to be significantly less important to highly motivated early adopters using a beta product than it will be once you're trying to attract a larger, more mainstream market. Early adopters forgive a lot, but they're more likely to forgive ugly than hard to use, so concentrate on making it easy and useful first, and make it pretty later.

How Much Visual Design Do YOU Need?

Lean UX has a well-deserved reputation for focusing on things that convert well over things that look good. In other words, if you've got a gorgeous new redesign that everybody loves the look of but that decreases your sales by 20%, Lean UX is going to insist that you change that gorgeous visual design to something that doesn't lose you money.

And that makes perfect sense. You're running a business, not a museum. The most gorgeous visual design in the world isn't worth what you're paying your designer if it doesn't improve conversion.

That said, Lean UX does not require that your product be ugly. The truth is that some types of products require a much higher level of visual design than others in order to convert well. You need to keep this in mind when figuring out how much effort to put into your visuals.

Let's say you've got a product that solves a severe problem for general contractors. Imagine that you don't have any serious competition in this particular space, and you're selling directly to the contractors with a dedicated sales force. Now let's say instead that you're creating a flash sale site for extremely upscale handbags. You're relying on social sharing to drive customer acquisition.

Which product do you think is going to need a higher quality visual design?

You see, good visual design can improve trust and encourage interaction. Better looking products can make people who stumble across them feel safer and more comfortable interacting with them. If you release some sort of high-price-point e-commerce site with a cheesy visual design, you're not going to move a lot of handbags, mostly because consumers in this space have a huge number of choices, and they expect a certain level of visual appeal.

On the other hand, visual design often has very little to do with purchasing decisions for complex enterprise products that solve serious business problems. In those cases, users are more likely to buy products based on how much they benefit the business. The vast majority of businesses would rather buy something that they think will save them money instead of something they think is pretty.

Is this the go-ahead to make your enterprise software hideous? Not really. It's important to realize that the line between enterprise products and consumer products is constantly blurring. After all, those corporate folks who are staring at your ugly product at work are playing with their iPads at home.

People are getting used to products that are uncluttered and easy to use. Even business users almost never expect to need a user manual these days. But when a product solves a serious problem for somebody that they simply can't get solved anywhere else, visual design becomes far less important.

As with any changes you're making to your product, when you spend time and money on visual design, you're trading off other things you'd be able to build. You have to figure out how much of a return on your investment you're getting.

In the case of a high-end flash sale site, the return on a sophisticated visual design can be quite high if it helps instill trust and encourages people to make a purchase. In the case of an enterprise product, or really any product that solves a serious problem for people that they can't get solved in any other way, the return may simply not be there.

As with all design decisions, you need to make sure you're testing as well as you can so that you can truly understand what sort of return you're getting for your visual design dollar.

Using Visual Design to Enhance Usability

A big part of any user experience design is figuring out where to put stuff. This may sound obvious, but it's best to put stuff where people are most likely to use it. That means associating calls-to-action with the thing that is being acted upon.

Here's an example you may have considered: Where do you put a buy button on a page? Well, when a user is trying to decide whether or not to buy something, which pieces of information is the user most likely to need? He definitely needs to know how much he's paying for the item. He might need pictures of the item. He almost certainly needs to know the name of the item and perhaps a short description.

Considering those needs, the buy button should probably go near those things on the page. It should even go in a defined visual area with just those things. Here's the hard part: It needs to go near those things *even if it looks better someplace else.*

Look, I'm all for having a nice visual design. I believe that a page should be balanced and pretty and have a reasonable amount of white space and all that. But if one element of your gorgeous visual design has separated your buy button from the information your user needs in order to decide to buy, then your gorgeous visual design is costing you more money than you think.

This isn't just true for buy buttons; it's true anytime the user has to make a decision. The call-to-action to make the decision must be visually associated with any information that the user needs to make that decision. Additionally, any information that is *not* related to the decision should be visually separate.

This also applies to things that aren't calls-to-action, of course. Related information should all be grouped together, while unrelated information should be somewhere else. It's just that simple. Oh, and bonus points if you keep all similar items in the same place on every screen of your product so people always know where to look.

The Smartest Visual Design You Can Do

I was speaking with an entrepreneur the other day who told me a relevant story. Apparently, she had spent time on visual polish for a login screen. There were a few things that took a while to implement, but they made the screen look much better. Unfortunately, the next week she had to rip it all out to change the feature, and all that time pushing pixels was wasted.

On the other hand, I've heard dozens of people talk about gorgeous and delightful interfaces from products like Path and Mint. Would they have gotten that kind of buzz without spending time on the visual details? Most likely not.

So what does this mean for you? Should you spend time on pixel-perfect screens and delightful visual design? No. And yes.

Here's what you should do: Spend a little time developing clean, flexible, easy-to-implement visual design standards.

It's probably not worth your time to fret and sweat over every single pixel on every single new page, mostly because you should always plan on iterating. When you're a startup, any new feature may be killed or transformed in a week's time.

If you spend days getting everything lined up beautifully on a product detail page, that could all be blown to hell as soon as you add something like Related Products or Comments.

Many people think that the right answer is to have a grand vision of everything that will eventually go on the page, but things change far too rapidly for this. Imagine that you've carefully designed a tabbed interface with just enough room for four tabs. Now imagine that you need to add a fifth tab. I hope you didn't spend too many hours getting all that spacing exactly right.

What You Should Do Instead

How about spending time on the basics that won't have to change every time you add a feature?

For example, you could establish standards for things like the following:

- An attractive color palette
- Font sizes and color standards for headers, subheaders, and body text
- Column sizes in grid layouts
- A simple and appealing icon set
- Standards for things like boxes, gradients, backgrounds, and separators
- A flexible header and footer design

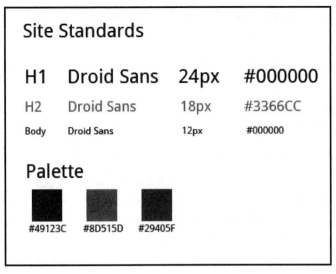

Figure 10-3. Don't let your engineers pick their own colors

Why you should do this

The great thing about having standards like these is that engineers can often combine them with sketches to implement decent-looking screens without having to go through a visual design phase at all.

Also, since these things are reusable and flexible, there's no wasted effort in creating them. Killing a feature doesn't make knowing that your H1s should be a certain size and color any less valuable.

The best part is that you save time in a few important ways. First, as I mentioned, you don't necessarily need to involve a visual designer every time you want to create a new screen.

Second, this sort of approach tends to encourage a much simpler, cleaner, more flexible design, since items need to work in various combinations. And lastly, it tends to keep things more consistent across your product, which means that you're less likely to have to go back later and do a complete redesign after things have gotten hideously out of whack.

A set of design standards won't solve all your visual design woes, but it will make developing new features go faster, and you won't be quite as sad when the new features fail miserably and you have to kill them.

Loosely Related Rant: The Best Visual Design in the World

As I've mentioned, I don't do visual design. It's not that I don't think it's important. I'm just not very good at it.

Even though I can't produce gorgeous visual designs, just like every other person on the planet I know what sorts of visual design I prefer. I don't have one particular style that I'm in love with, but I have pretty strong reactions, both positive and negative, to different "looks."

Recently, I worked with a company that had a visual design I didn't like. Now, since I'm not a visual designer, I'm not going to speculate on whether it was badly designed or just not to my taste, but I will tell you that when I showed it to many people in Silicon Valley, they didn't like it either.

In fact, enough people reacted negatively that I stopped showing it to people in the Valley. I even found myself apologizing for it, despite the fact that I didn't design it, and I don't love it.

And then I did some user testing on the site. And do you know what? The users loved it. They *loved* it. It was absolutely fantastic for this particular demographic, which, by the way, had nothing to do with the Silicon Valley CEOs and designers who were horrified by it.

I was showing some wireframes, with the usual disclaimers of "This isn't how it will look; these are just black-and-white mockups of the final site; we're not losing the other color scheme." Despite repeated statements to this effect, users would periodically interrupt the test to volunteer how much they loved the visual design of the site and how they really didn't want it to change.

Why is this important? It's a great example of the fact that your visual design should reflect the aesthetic of your target market and not you. Say it with me, "You are not your user."

Designing a beautiful, elegant, slick site that will appeal to designers, Silicon Valley executives, and Apple users is fantastic...if you're selling to designers, Silicon Valley executives, or Apple users. That wasn't the market for this company, so it was smart to build a product that appealed to its own market instead.

Is there such a thing as bad visual design? Sure. I've certainly seen visual designs that interfered with usability. Buttons can be too small; calls-to-action can be de-emphasized; screens can be too cluttered; navigation can be hard to find. But just because something isn't visually appealing to you doesn't make it a bad visual design. The only people who have to like it are your users.

In your next design meeting, remember this: The best visual design in the world is the one your users love.

Go Do This Now!

- Understand what your users expect: Try having a conversation with some of your regular users about some of their favorite products. Ask them why they like the ones they like. You may be surprised how many love really ugly but useful things.

- Make a visual standards guide: Try going through your product and listing things like fonts, colors, and button treatments that you're currently using. Now put this list where everybody who codes can easily access it and ask them to try to reuse visual styles whenever possible.

- Prioritize function over form: The next time you find yourself tempted to make something more difficult to use just because it looks better, try stopping and thinking about what that's really going to do to your key metrics. Will you lose customers because of it? Will you lose money? Is it really worth it?

PART THREE:

PRODUCT

I hate to be the one to break it to you, but User Experience Design doesn't end when you ship your product. Even if you do everything else in this book right, you still won't know what your actual user experience is going to be like until you have a real product in the hands of real users.

In the first two sections, we talked about validating your ideas, understanding your customers, creating designs, and avoiding waste.

This last section deals with Lean methods of understanding and improving the real customer experience of your product, as well as some ways to improve your own development process.

Of course, the section is going to cover metrics. Metrics are at the heart of Lean Startup and Lean UX. This section will talk about ways to measure design intelligently and not fall into some dangerous data traps.

This section also goes into some general-purpose tips for making your entire team more Lean and efficient. It may not be immediately clear how that relates to UX, but in my experience, Agile, iterative, efficient teams create better user experiences every time.

CHAPTER 11

Measure It!

In this chapter:

- Learn how to measure how much your UX changes are helping your business.

- Understand how to use A/B testing in conjunction with good UX practices to get great design outcomes and avoid local maxima.

- Learn how to successfully combine qualitative and quantitative research methods.

- Figure out how to avoid the most common pitfalls of using data to make product decisions.

- See which metrics you can use to measure user happiness.

I've talked a lot about qualitative research. But let's step back and talk about quantitatively measuring design for a minute.

This is a topic that angers a lot of designers. If you are one of them, I'm going to ask that you bear with me. Measuring design results is a great thing. It can be incredibly helpful to you as a designer, and it's even more helpful to the company.

But don't just accept my word for it. Let's break it down. If you still don't agree with me at the end of the chapter, then write your own damn book and prove me wrong.

What Does Measuring Design Entail, Anyway?

Typically, when I'm talking about measuring design results, I'm talking about A/B testing.

For those of you who aren't familiar with the practice, A/B testing (sometimes called bucket testing or multivariate testing) is the practice of creating multiple versions of a screen or feature and showing each version to a different set of users in production in order to find out which version produces better metrics.

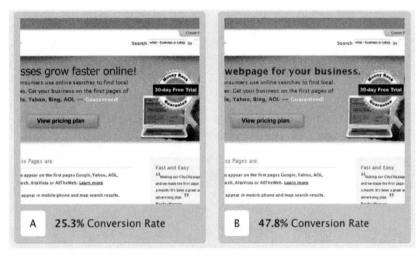

Figure 11-1. Even small copy changes can make a difference

These metrics may include things like "Which version of a new feature makes the company more money?" or "Which landing screen positively affects conversion?" Overall, the goal of A/B testing is to allow you to make better product decisions based on the things that are important to your business by using statistically significant data.

There are other types of analytics that you may have heard of, but this chapter is going to deal exclusively with this type of comparative testing. Controlled A/B testing of this sort is the only way to truly understand the impact that changes have on behavior.

Think of A/B testing like a science experiment. You always need a control group to measure against, or you have no way of knowing what would have happened if you hadn't made your change.

Why Measure Design?

So now you know technically what testing means. Why would you bother to do it?

The single best reason for measuring design is to understand if what you are doing is making a difference, positive or negative, to your company. You'll note I said "company" and not "users" or "product." There's a reason for that.

I'm going to assume that you are in business to make money. I'm also going to assume that you would like most of the things that you spend a lot of time and effort on to make it more likely that you will make money. For my last assumption, I'm going to say that you would like to know what things you want to do more of and what things you want to stop doing.

If you feel these are not reasonable assumptions, then feel free to skip to the next chapter.

Quite simply, measuring your design efforts helps you understand whether the changes you make to your product help or hurt your bottom line. If you do it correctly, you can find out really important things like, "That new visual redesign on the checkout flow improved purchase completion by 10%." Or "The search feature caused people to spend 20% more money." Or "That visual design we spent so much money on didn't affect user behavior at all."

You'll note that testing doesn't tell you what you should do about any of those situations. It doesn't tell you that you have to scrap the new visual design. It might help inform your decision making in the future when somebody suggests doing a huge, expensive new visual redesign.

You see, measuring design isn't about giving up your design aesthetic or just testing everything and seeing what sticks. It's about using solid research and great design skills to create new features and then testing to see whether they helped.

That said, I frequently hear the same old arguments against testing design. Let's take a look at some of those.

Several Stupid Reasons for Not A/B Testing (and a Couple of Good Ones)

I think a big part of the pushback against A/B testing is a fundamental misunderstanding of the right way to use A/B testing.

Look, A/B testing is a tool. Sometimes people use it poorly or for things it wasn't meant to solve. The fact that A/B testing fails in these cases is not the fault of A/B testing. Don't blame a hammer for sucking at sawing boards in half.

Here are some of the (mostly bad) reasons that people give me for not doing A/B testing.

It Takes Away the Need for Design

For some reason, people think that A/B testing means that you just randomly test whatever crazy shit pops into your head. They envision a world where engineers algorithmically generate feature ideas, build them all, and then just measure which one does best.

This is absolute nonsense.

A/B testing only specifies that you need to test new designs against each other or against some sort of a control. It says absolutely zero about how you come up with those design ideas.

As I've pointed out repeatedly in this book, the best way to come up with great features and products people love to use is to go out and observe those users and find problems that you can solve and then use good design processes to solve them. When you start testing, you're not changing anything at all about that process. You're just making sure that you get metrics on how those changes affect real user behavior.

Let's imagine that you're building an online site to buy pet food. You come up with a fabulous landing page idea that involves some sort of talking sock puppet. You decide to create this puppet character based on your intimate knowledge of your user base and your sincere belief that what they are missing in their lives is a talking sock puppet. It's a reasonable assumption.

Instead of just launching your wholly reimagined landing page, complete with talking sock puppet video, you create your landing page and show it to only half of your users, while the rest of your users are stuck with their sad, sock puppet–less version of the site. Then you look to see which group of users bought more pet food.

It's really that simple. Nothing about A/B testing determines *what* you're going to test. It has literally nothing to do with the initial design and research process. You can test anything.

You can even test entire features. You could release a product page that showed comments to only half the visitors in order to understand whether commenting affected purchase and retention rates.

Whatever you're testing, you still need somebody who is good at creating the experiences you're planning on testing against each other. A/B testing two crappy experiences does, in fact, lead to a final crappy experience. After all, if you're looking at two options that both suck, A/B testing is going to determine only which one sucks less.

Design is still incredibly important. It just becomes possible to measure design's impact with A/B testing.

It's Useful Only for Small Changes

I know, I know. Google tested the shades of blue. That's not the only thing that A/B testing is good for.

Figure 11-2. Not the only use for A/B testing

The Google test to find the best color of blue for links is famous, but it's only useful when you're trying to get people to click on links at an enormous scale.

The thing is, A/B testing in no way limits testing to things like link colors or button text, although it can be really nice for that. As I already mentioned, A/B testing can be used for adding entirely new features or for massive, product-wide changes.

I don't know any other way to counter this argument than just explaining that A/B testing has literally nothing to do with the size of the change.

It Leads to Local Maxima

This argument is very similar to the previous one. It's basically the idea that, while A/B testing will improve what you have, it won't let you find much bigger opportunities.

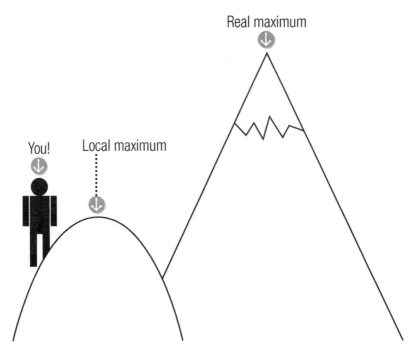

Figure 11-3. Reaching a local maximum

Climbing to the top of the hill you're on gets you higher, but it doesn't always maximize your altitude. Sometimes you need to find a taller hill.

I've always found this to be a particularly annoying argument, because truthfully A/B testing doesn't even improve what you have.

A/B testing tests. It's agnostic about what you're testing. If you're just testing small changes, you'll get only small changes. This means you're likely to optimize yourself to a local maxima.

If, on the other hand, you test big things—major navigation changes, new features, new purchasing flows, completely different products—then you'll get big changes.

Once again, the fact that you're A/B testing has literally nothing to do with the size of things you can be testing, so it doesn't necessarily lead to local maxima.

It Leads to a Confused Mess of an Interface

Anybody who has looked at Amazon's product pages recently knows the sort of thing that A/B testing can lead to. Those pages have a huge amount of information on them, and none of it seems particularly well designed or attractive.

On the other hand, they rake in money.

It's true that when you're doing lots of A/B testing on various features, you can wind up with a weird mishmash of things in your product that don't necessarily create a harmonious overall design.

As an example, let's say you're testing your own product detail page. You decide to run several A/B tests for the following features:

- Customer photos
- Comments
- Ratings
- Product details
- Extended product details
- Shipping information
- Information about the manufacturer
- Normal price
- Sale price
- Return info

Now let's imagine that each one of those items, in its own A/B test, increases conversion by some small but statistically significant margin. Now you've got a product detail page with a huge number of things on it. You might, rightly, worry that the page is becoming so overwhelming that you'll actually start to lose conversions.

Again, this is not the fault of A/B testing—or in this case, A/B/C/D/E testing. This is the fault of a bad test.

You see, it's not enough that you run an A/B test. You have to run a good A/B test. In this case, you might be better off running several sequential tests rather than trying to run a test with everything at once.

For example, start your baseline product detail page with the bare number of things that you know you need to sell a product: a price, a picture, a buy button, a name for the product. Now add something to it—for example, some customer photos. Did it increase conversion in a statistically significant way? Great! Keep it and try adding another thing. Repeat.

If you're already at the point where you've got an overwhelming amount of information, try removing a few of the items and seeing how it affects your conversion.

I wish I could tell you exactly which items are going to convert well for you, but the fact is, it's different for every product. Sometimes seeing customer photos will be the key. Sometimes learning more about the construction of the item will be incredibly important. Sometimes social proof that your friends all like a product will make the difference.

This is why you test—so you don't have to guess whether adding or removing a feature improves your conversion. And if you end up with a page that looks like the Amazon product detail page, well, as long as you also have its conversion rate, maybe it's not such a bad thing.

Design Isn't About Metrics

This is the argument that infuriates me the most. I have literally heard people say that we shouldn't measure design, because design isn't about the bottom line. It's about the customer experience.

This is complete nonsense.

Look, imagine using Amazon again. Wouldn't it be a better experience if everything were free? Be honest! It totally would. Unfortunately, it would be a somewhat traumatic experience for the Amazon stockholders.

You see, we don't always optimize for the absolute best user experience. We make tradeoffs constantly. We aim for a fabulous user experience that also delivers fabulous profits.

While it's true that we don't want to just turn our user experience design over to short-term revenue metrics, I believe that we can vastly improve user experience by seeing which improvements and features are most beneficial for both users and the company.

Design is not art. If you think that there's some ideal design that is completely divorced from the effect it's having on your company's bottom line, then you're an artist, not a designer. Design has a purpose and a goal, and those things can be measured.

By measuring design, we can see how the changes we make really affect user behavior and how they contribute to the company's bottom line. I, for one, think that's marvelous. If you disagree, that's entirely your prerogative, but don't expect to be hired by Lean startups.

When to A/B Test and When to Research

So we spent the first part of the book talking about qualitative research and the last few pages talking about quantitative. While they're both types of research, it's critical that you understand when you should use each one.

Both A/B testing and qualitative research are great for helping you make better product decisions based on feedback. But they answer entirely different questions. Using them together, you can answer far more types of questions than you can using only one alone.

In fact, qualitative user research combined with A/B testing creates the most powerful system for informing design that I have ever seen. If you're not doing it yet, you should be.

What A/B Testing Does Well

A/B testing on its own is fantastic for certain things. It can help you do the following:

- Get statistically significant data on whether a proposed new feature or change significantly increases metrics that matter—numbers like revenue, retention, and customer acquisition.

- Understand more about what your customers are actually doing on your site.

- Make decisions about which features to cut and which to improve.

- Validate design decisions.

- See which small changes have surprisingly large effects on metrics.

- Get user feedback without actually interacting with users.

For example, imagine that you are creating a new checkout flow for your website. There is a request from your marketing department to include an extra screen that asks users for some demographic information. However, you feel that every additional step in a checkout process represents a chance for users to drop out, which prevents purchases.

By creating two flows in production, one with the extra screen and one without, and showing each flow to only half of your users, you can gather real data on how many purchases are completed by members of each group. This allows you to understand the exact impact on sales and helps you decide whether gathering the demographic information is really worth the cost.

Even more appealing, you can get all this user feedback without ever talking to a single user. A/B testing is, by its nature, an engineering solution to a product design problem, which makes it very popular with small, engineering-driven teams. Once the various versions of the feature are released to users, almost anybody can look at the results and understand which option is doing better, so it can all be done without having to recruit or interview test participants.

Of course, A/B testing in production works best on things like web or mobile applications, where you can not only show different interfaces to different customers, but you can also easily switch all of your users to the winning interface without having to ship them a new box full of software or a new physical device. I wouldn't recommend trying it if you're designing, for example, a car.

What It Does Poorly

Now imagine that, instead of adding a single screen to an existing check-out flow, you are tasked with designing an entirely new checkout flow that should maximize revenue and minimize the number of people who abandon their shopping carts. In creating the new flow, there are hundreds of design decisions you need to make, both small and large. How many screens should it have? How much up-selling and cross-selling should you do? At what point in the flow do you ask users for payment information? What should the screens look like? Should they have the standard header and footer, or should those be removed to minimize potential distractions for users when purchasing? And on and on and on...

These are all just a series of small decisions, so, in an ideal world, you'd be able to A/B test each one separately, right? Of course, in the real world, this could mean creating an A/B test with hundreds of different variations, each of which has to be shown to enough users to achieve statistical significance. Since you want to roll out your new checkout process sometime before the next century, this may not be a particularly appealing option.

A Bad Solution

Another option would be to fully implement several very different directions for the checkout screens and test them all against one another. For example, let's say you implemented four different checkout processes with the following features to test against one another.

OPTION 1	OPTION 2	OPTION 3	OPTION 4
Yellow Background	Blue Background	Orange Background	White Background
Three Screens	Two Screens	Four Screens	One Screen
Marketing Questions	No Marketing Questions	Marketing Questions	No Marketing Questions
No Up-selling	Up-selling	Up-selling	No Up-selling
No Cross-selling	No Cross-selling	Cross-selling	Cross-selling
Header	Header	No Header	No Header
No Footer	Footer	Footer	No Footer
Help Link	No Help	Live Chat Help	Live Chat Help

Figure 11-4. Four checkout-flow design combinations

This might work in companies that have lots of bored engineers sitting around waiting to implement and test several different versions of the same code, most of which will eventually be thrown away. Frankly, I haven't run across a lot of those companies.

But even if you did decide to devote the resources to building four different checkout flows, the big problem is that, if you get a clear winner, you really don't have a very clear idea of *why* users preferred a particular version of the checkout flow. Sure, you can make educated guesses. Perhaps it was the particularly soothing shade of blue. Or maybe it was the fact that there weren't any marketing questions. Or maybe it was aggressive up-selling. Or maybe that version just had the fewest bugs.

Unless you figure out exactly which parts users liked and which they didn't like, it's impossible to know that you're maximizing your revenue. It's also impossible to use that data to improve other parts of your site. After all, what if people *hate* the soothing shade of blue, but they like everything else about the new checkout process? Think of all the money you'll lose by not going with the yellow or orange or white. Think of all the time you'll waste by making everything else on your site that particular shade of blue, since you think you've statistically proven that people love it!

What Qualitative Testing Does Well

Despite the many wonderful things about A/B testing, there are a few things that qualitative testing just does better.

Find the Best of All Worlds

When you are testing wildly different versions of a feature against one another, qualitative testing allows you to understand what works about each of them, thereby helping you develop a solution that has the best parts from all the different options.

This is especially useful when designing complicated features that require many individual decisions, any one of which might have a significant impact on metrics. By observing users interacting with the different versions, you can begin to understand the pros and cons of each small piece of the design without having to run each one individually in its own A/B test.

Find Out Why Users Are Leaving

While a good A/B test (or plain-old analytics) can tell you which page a user is on when he abandons a checkout flow, it can't tell you why he left. Did he get confused? Bored? Stuck? Distracted? Information like that helps you make better decisions about what exactly it is on the page that is causing people to leave, and watching people using your feature is the best way to gather that information.

Save Engineering Time and Iterate Faster

Generally, qualitative tests are run with rich, interactive wireframes rather than fully designed and tested code. This means that, instead of having your engineers code and test four different versions of the flow, you can have a designer create four different HTML prototypes in a fraction of the time.

And since making changes to a prototype doesn't require any engineering or QA time, you can iterate on the design much faster, allowing you to refine the design in hours or days rather than weeks or months.

How Do They Work Together?

Qualitative Testing Narrows Down What You Need to A/B Test

Qualitative testing will let you eliminate the obviously confusing stuff, confirm the obviously good stuff, and narrow down the set of features you want to A/B test to a more manageable size. There will still be questions that are best answered by statistics, but there will be a lot fewer of them.

Remember our matrix of four different checkout flows? Qualitative testing can help eliminate the ones that are clearly not working or that cause significant usability problems. You might still have a couple of different versions of the page that you want to test against each other, but there will be significantly fewer options once you've gotten rid of the ones that were destined to fail.

Qualitative Testing Generates New Ideas for Features and Designs

While A/B testing can help you eliminate features or designs that clearly aren't working, it can't give you new ideas. Users can. If every user you interview gets stuck in the same place, you've identified a new problem to solve. If users are unenthusiastic about a particular feature, you can explore what's missing with them and come up with new ways to make the product more engaging.

Talking to your users allows you to create a hypothesis that you can then validate with an A/B test. For example, maybe all the users you interviewed about your checkout flow got stuck selecting a shipment method. To address this, you might come up with ideas for a couple of new shipment flows that you can test in production (once you've confirmed that they're less confusing with another quick qualitative test).

A/B Testing Creates a Feedback Loop for Researchers

A/B tests can also improve your qualitative testing process by providing statistical feedback to your designers. I, as a designer, am going to observe participants during tests in order to see what they like and dislike. I'm then going to make some educated guesses about how to improve the product based on my observations.

When I get feedback about which designs are the most successful, it helps me learn more about what's important to users so I make better designs in the future.

Not Sold Yet?

Separately, both A/B testing and qualitative testing are great ways to learn more about your users and how they interact with your product. Combined, they are more than the sum of their parts. They form an incredibly powerful tool that can help you make good, user-centered product decisions more quickly and with more confidence than you have ever imagined.

Which Metrics Equal Happy Users

We've spent a lot of time in this chapter talking about A/B testing, but there are other types of metrics and analytics that are available to you. Many of these can help you improve your user experience exponentially, but only if used correctly.

In fact, one of the greatest tools available to me as an interaction designer is the ability to see real metrics. I'm guessing that's surprising to some people. After all, many people still think that design all happens before a product ever gets into the hands of users, so how could I possibly benefit from finding out what users are really doing with my products?

Well, for one thing, I believe that design should continue for as long as a product is being used by or sold to customers. As I have mentioned about a thousand times already in this book, design is an iterative process, and there's nothing that gives me quicker, more accurate insight into how a new product version or feature is performing than looking at user metrics.

But there's something that I, as a user advocate, care about quite a lot that is very hard to measure accurately. I care about user happiness.

Now, I don't necessarily care about happiness for some vague, good-karma reason. I care because I think that happy users are retained users and, often, paying users. I believe that happy users tell their friends about my product and reduce my acquisition costs. I truly believe that happy users mean more money for me in the long run.

So how can I tell whether my users are happy? You know, without talking to every single one of them?

Although I think that happy users can equal more registrations, more revenue, and more retention, I don't actually believe that this implies the opposite. Customers can be quite unhappy while still signing up for and using my product.

In fact, there are all sorts of things I can do to retain customers or to get more money out of them that don't make them happy. The following examples are a few of the important business metrics you might be tempted to use as shorthand for customer happiness...but it's not always the case.

Retention

An increase in retention numbers seems like a good indication that your customers are happy. After all, happier customers stay longer, right? We just established that.

But do you mean retention or forced retention? I can artificially increase my retention numbers by locking new users into a long contract, and that's going to keep them with me for a while. Once that contract's up, of course, they are free to move wherever they like, and then I need to acquire a customer to replace them. And, if my contract is longer than my competitors' contracts, it can scare off new users.

Also, the retention metric is easy to affect with switching barriers, which may increase the number of months I have a customer while making him less happy. Of course, if those switching barriers are removed for any reason—for example, cell phone number portability—I can lose my hold over those previously retained customers.

While retention can be an indicator of happy customers, increasing retention by any means necessary doesn't necessarily make your customers happier.

Revenue

Revenue's another metric that seems like it would point to happy customers. Increased revenue means people are spending more, which means they like the service!

Except that there are all sorts of ways I can increase my revenue without making my customers happier. For example, I can rope them into paying for things they didn't ask for or use deceptive strategies to get them to sign up for expensive subscriptions. This can work in the short term, but it's likely to make some customers very unhappy, and maybe make them ex-customers (or lawsuit plaintiffs) in the long run.

Revenue is also tricky to judge for free or ad-supported products. Again, you can boost ad revenue on a site simply by piling more ads onto a page, but that doesn't necessarily enhance your users' experience or happiness.

While increased revenue may indicate that people are spending more because they find your product more appealing, it can also be caused by sacrificing long-term revenue for short-term gains.

NPS (Net Promoter Score)

The net promoter score is a measure of how many of your users would recommend your product to a friend. It's actually a pretty good measure of customer happiness, but the problem is that it can be tricky to gauge accurately. It generally needs to be obtained through surveys and customer contact rather than simple analytics, so it suffers from relying on self-reported data and small sample sizes. Also, it tends to be skewed in favor of the type of people who answer surveys and polls, which may or may not be representative of your customer base.

While NPS may be the best indicator of customer happiness, it can be difficult to collect accurately. Unless your sample size is quite large, the variability from week to week can make it tough to see smaller changes that may warn of a coming trend.

Conversion to Paying

For products using the freemium or browsing model, this can be a useful metric, since it lets you know that people like your free offering enough to pay for more. However, it can take awhile to collect the data after you make a change to your product because you have to wait for enough new users to convert to payers.

Also, it doesn't work well on ad-supported products or products that require payment up front.

Most importantly, it doesn't let you know how happy your paying customers are, since they've already converted.

Conversion to paying can be useful, but it is limited to freemium or browsing models, and it tends to skew toward measuring the free part of the product rather than the paid product.

Engagement

Engagement is an interesting metric to study, since it tells me how soon and how often users are electing to come back to interact with the product and how long they're spending.

This can definitely be one of the indicators of customer happiness for e-commerce, social networking, or gaming products that want to maximize the amount of time spent by each user. However, increasing engagement for a utility product like processing payroll or managing personal information might actually be an indicator that users are being forced to do more work than they'd like.

Also, engagement is one of the easiest metrics to manipulate in the short run. One-time efforts, like marketing campaigns, special offers, or prize giveaways can temporarily increase engagement, but unless they're sustainable and cost effective, they're not going to contribute to the long-term happiness of your customers.

For example, one company I worked with tried inflating its engagement numbers by offering prizes for coming back repeatedly for the first few days. While this did get people to return after their first visit, it didn't have any effect on long-term user happiness or adoption rates.

Engagement can be one factor in determining customer happiness, but this may not apply if you don't have an entertainment or shopping product. Also, make sure your engagement numbers are being driven by customer enjoyment of your product and not by artificial tricks.

Registration

While registration can be the fastest metric to see changes in, it's basically worthless for figuring out how happy your users are, since they're not interacting with the product until after they've registered. The obvious exception is products with delayed (i.e., lazy) registration, in which case it can act like a lower-barrier-to-entry version of conversion to paying.

When you allow users to use your product for a while before committing, an increase in registration can mean that users are finding your product compelling enough to take the next step and register.

Registration is an indicator of happy customers only when it's lazy, and even then it's only a piece of the puzzle, albeit an important one.

Customer Service Contacts

You'd think that decreasing the number of calls and emails to your customer service team would give you a pretty good idea of how happy your customers are. Unfortunately, this one can be manipulated aggressively by nasty tactics like making it harder to get to a representative or to find a phone number. A sudden decrease in the number of support calls might mean that people are having far fewer problems. Or it might mean that people have given up trying to contact you and have gone somewhere else.

Decreased customer service contacts may be caused by happier customers, but that's not always the case.

So Which Is It?

While all of these metrics can be extremely important to your business, no single metric can tell you if you are making your customers happy. However, looking at trends in all of them can certainly help you determine whether a recent change to your product has made your customers happier.

For example, imagine that you introduce a new element to your social networking site that reminds users of their friends' birthdays and then helps them choose and buy the perfect gifts. Before you release the feature, you decide that it is likely to positively affect the following:

Engagement

Every time you send a reminder of a birthday, it gives the user a reason to come back to the product and reengage.

Revenue

Assuming you are taking a cut of the gift revenue, you should see an increase when people find and buy presents.

Conversion to paying

You're giving your users a new reason to spend money.

(Lazy) Registration

If you allow only registered users to take advantage of the new feature, this can give people a reason to register.

You're giving users a reason to stay with you and keep coming back year after year, since people keep having birthdays.

Once the feature is released, you look at those numbers and see a statistically significant positive movement in all or most of those metrics.

As long as the numbers aren't being inflated by tricks or unsustainable methods (for example, you're selling the gifts at a huge loss, or you're giving people extra birthdays), you can assume that your customers are being made happy by your new feature and that the feature will have a positive impact on your business.

Of course, while you're looking at all your numbers and metrics and analysis, some good old-fashioned customer outreach, where you get out and talk directly with users, can also do wonders for your understanding of *why* they're feeling the way they're feeling.

Loosely Related Rant: Stupid Mistakes People Make When Analyzing Data

It doesn't do any good for me to go on and on about all the ways you can gather critical data if people don't know how to analyze that data once you have it.

I would have thought that a lot of this stuff was obvious, but, judging from my experience working with many different companies, it's not. Analyzing the data you've gathered is apparently really hard, and everybody seems to make the exact same mistakes over and over.

All the examples here are real mistakes I've seen made by smart, reasonable, employed people. A few identifying characteristics have been changed to protect the innocent, but in general they were product owners, managers, or director-level folks.

Just to be clear, the quantitative data to which I'm referring is typically generated by the following types of activities:

- Multivariate or A/B testing

- Site analytics

- Business metrics reports (sales, revenue, registration, etc.)

- Large-scale surveys

Statistical Significance

I see this one all the time. It generally involves somebody saying something like, "We tested two different landing pages against each other. Out of six hundred views, one of them had three conversions and one had six. That means the second one is *twice as good*! We should switch to it immediately!"

OK, I may be exaggerating a bit on the actual numbers, but too many people I've worked with just ignored the statistical significance of their data. They didn't realize that even very large numbers can be statistically insignificant, depending on the sample size.

The problem here is that statistically insignificant metrics can completely reverse themselves, so it's important not to make changes based on results until you are reasonably certain that those results are predictable and repeatable.

The fix

I was going to go into a long description of statistical significance and how to calculate it, but then I realized that, if you don't know what it is, you shouldn't be trying to make decisions based on quantitative data.

There are online calculators that will help you figure out if any particular test result is statistically significant, but make sure that whoever is looking at your data understands basic statistical concepts before accepting their interpretation.

Also, a word of warning: Testing several branches of changes can take a *lot* larger sample size than a simple A/B test. If you're running an A/B/C/D/E test, make sure you understand the mathematical implications.

Short-Term versus Long-Term Effects

Again, this seems so obvious that I feel weird stating it, but I've seen people get so excited over short-term changes that they totally ignore the effects of their changes in a week or a month or a year. The best, but not only, example of this is when people try to judge the effect of certain types of sales promotions on revenue.

For example, I've often heard something along these lines, "When we ran the 50% off sale, our revenue *skyrocketed*!" Sure it did. What happened to your revenue after the sale ended? My guess is that it plummeted, since people had already stocked up on your product at 50% off.

The fix

Does this mean you should never run a short-term promotion of any sort? Of course not. What it does mean is that, when you are looking at the results of any sort of experiment or change, you should look at how it affects your metrics over time.

Forgetting the Goal of the Metrics

Sometimes people get so focused on the metrics that they forget that the metrics are just shorthand for real-world business goals. They can end up trying so hard to move a particular metric that they sacrifice the actual goal.

Here's another real-life example: One client decided that, since revenue was directly tied to people returning to its site after an initial visit, it was going to "encourage" people to come back for a second look. This was fine as far as it went, but after various tests it found that the most successful way to get people to return was to give them a gift every time they did.

The unsurprising result was that the people who just came back for the gift didn't end up converting to paying customers. The company moved the "returning" metric without affecting the "revenue" metric, which had been the real goal in the first place. Additionally, it now had the added cost of supporting more nonpaying users on the site, so it ended up costing money.

The fix

Don't forget the business goals behind your metrics, and don't get stuck on what Eric Ries calls "vanity metrics." Remember to consider the secondary effects of your metrics. Increasing your traffic comes with certain costs, so make sure that you are getting something other than more traffic out of your traffic increase!

Combining Data from Multiple Tests

Sometimes you want to test different changes independently of one another, and that's often a good thing, since it can help you determine which change had an effect on a particular metric. However, this can be dangerous if used stupidly.

Consider this somewhat ridiculous thought experiment. Imagine you have a landing page that is gray with a light-gray call-to-action button. Let's say you run two separate experiments. In one, you change the background color of the page to red so that you have a light-gray button on a red background. In another test, you change the call-to-action to red so that you have a red button on a gray background. Let's say that both of these convert better than the original page. Since you've tested both of your elements separately, and they're both better, you decide to implement both changes, leaving you with...a red call-to-action button on a red page. This will almost certainly not go well.

Figure 11-5. A + B shouldn't necessarily equal C

Just because red text and a red button won their separate A/B tests doesn't mean that red text on a red button is a winning combination.

The fix

Make sure that when you're combining the results from multiple tests that you still go back and test the final outcome against some control. In many cases, the whole is not the sum of its parts, and you can end up with an unholy mess if you don't use some common sense in interpreting data from various tests.

Understanding the Significance of Changes

This one just makes me sad. I've been in lots of meetings with product owners who described changes in the data for which they were responsible. Notice I said "described" and not "explained." Product owners would tell me, "Revenue increased" or "Retention went from 2 months to 1.5 months" or something along those lines. Obviously, my response was, "That's interesting. Why did it happen?"

You'd be shocked at how many product owners not only didn't know why their metrics were changing, but they didn't have a plan for figuring it out. The problem is, they were generating tons of charts showing increases and decreases, but they never really understood why the changes were happening, so they couldn't extrapolate from the experience to affect their metrics in a predictable way.

Even worse, sometimes they would make up hypotheses about why the metrics changed but not actually test them. For example, one product owner did a "Spend more than $10 and get a free gift" promo over a weekend. The weekend's sales were slightly higher than the previous weekend's sales, so she attributed that increase to the promotion. Unfortunately, a cursory look at the data showed that the percentage of people spending over $10 was no larger than it had been in previous weeks.

On the other hand, there had been far more people on the site than in pre-vious weeks due to seasonality and an unrelated increase in traffic. Based on the numbers, it was extremely unlikely that it was the promotion that increased revenue, but she didn't understand how to measure whether her changes actually made any difference.

The fix

Say it with me: "Correlation does not equal causation!" Whenever possible, test changes against a control so that you can accurately judge what effect they're having on specific metrics. If that's not possible, make sure that you understand ahead of time what changes you are *likely* to see from a particular change and then judge whether that happened. For example, a successful "spend more than $10 promo" should most likely increase the percentage of orders over $10.

Also, be aware of other changes within the company so that you can determine whether it was *your* change that affected your metrics. Anything from a school holiday to an increased ad spend might affect your numbers, so you need to know what to expect.

Go Do This Now!

- Take a look at your testing practices: If you're already A/B testing, try looking at your last few A/B tests. Are they likely to lead you to a local maximum? If so, try testing something bigger than button color or text.

- Understand what makes your users happy: Try setting up an NPS survey for your current users and track the information over several weeks. Follow up with unhappy customers to see what you're doing wrong.

CHAPTER 12

Go Faster!

In this chapter:

- Learn how cross-functional teams can move faster and react to user feedback better.

- Get tips on how to speed up your product development process without sacrificing quality.

Let's face it, you've got only so much time. Don't worry, this isn't some irritatingly existential meditation on the meaning of death. I'm not a harbinger of doom shrieking a warning about the mortality of mankind (except for that one Christmas party that I think we'd all prefer to forget).

Companies have limited resources, and startups tend to be more limited than most. We have to make trade-offs constantly. Building one feature can mean sacrificing half a dozen other equally promising opportunities.

Don't get me wrong. Making these decisions is really, really hard. These techniques will not make the decisions easy. They aren't even guaranteed to make them right. But they will make them faster. And that's almost as good.

The faster you can validate or invalidate hypotheses, the more things you can try before you run out of money. That can mean the difference between finding product market fit and finding a new job.

Here are some things you should be doing to make your UX faster. I've thrown in a few that don't seem to have much to do with UX. Speeding up the entire process means more iterations, and, when done right, more iterations mean a better product.

Work as a Cross-Functional Team

One of the hallmarks of Lean UX is not working in a waterfall style, where each group works independently of the others. This is a traditional method of producing products where the product manager starts everything off by writing a full spec for the product before passing the baton to design, which completes a full design process before finally allowing engineering to start work.

I'm not going to spend a huge amount of time explaining why it's slow and tends to be bad at producing innovative products. I'll just say that, having worked in both waterfall and Lean environments, there's a good reason I'm not writing a book called *UX for Waterfall Startups*. But seriously, read Eric Ries's *The Lean Startup* (Crown Business) for more info on this.

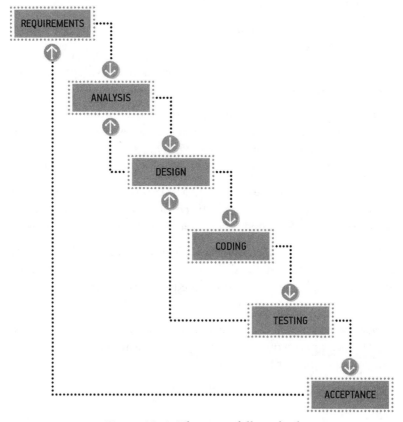

Figure 12-1. The waterfall method

The real question though, is what is the alternative? The best alternative is the cross-functional team.

This can be a tough change for people who are used to working in their own little silos, but combining people into one product team lets you go much faster. More importantly, it lets you be more flexible, so you can change directions and react quickly to user feedback and metrics.

Instead of setting up your organization with a User-Research Department, a User-Experience Department, a Product Department, and an Engineering Department, imagine having a team focused, for example, on the First-Time User Experience.

This team would include a few engineers, a product owner, and a designer, at a minimum. Other people, like customer service, QA, or sales, might also be involved with the group.

When deciding what projects to work on next, the team would all be involved from the beginning. So, for example, engineers would frequently sit in on user-research sessions and attend early feature discussions. Product owners and designers would conduct their user research together so that everybody would know exactly what problem they were solving. Designers would work closely with the engineers implementing their designs to make sure that any changes didn't affect the overall user experience negatively. They'd also be responsible for understanding the effect their changes had on metrics so that they could make small adjustments as necessary.

Let's look at a couple of examples, one with everyone in silos and the other with everyone on a cross-functional team.

The Waterfall

Imagine you're creating a new payment system, and by God, you're going to do it old school! That's right. All waterfall, all the time is your motto.

Fine. The first thing you're almost certainly going to do is to have some sort of product manager determine what exactly is getting built. If you're smart, that product manager may talk to some potential clients. But, more likely, the product manager will sit in a windowless room with a whiteboard and think about what payment systems are. She will then write these down in a specification document of some sort.

Often this can take weeks. In my experience, there are a lot of meetings and debates with other high-level people about all the features that will be required. The specification document is typically quite large.

If you're lucky, you've got a designer who can take those specifications and turn them into some pictures. Since the designer was rarely engaged in creating the business specifications, she's likely to just translate whatever is in the document into an attractive interface. She will, obviously, include all of the specified features, regardless of whether they make the interface better or not.

This can also take awhile. Sometimes weeks or months, depending on the size of the new product or feature. If you've hired an agency, chances are that the deliverable will be beautiful, which means that you paid thousands of dollars to create a gorgeous document that none of your users will ever see.

Once that's finished, there's a handoff to the engineering department. This is typically where everything goes to hell. Since the engineers haven't been involved in the process up until this point, this is where they start to point out that the thing they're supposed to build is going to take half the department about a thousand years.

Also, they're going to have to rewrite the entire backend because of a couple of features that the product manager felt were required.

By the way, if you think I'm exaggerating, you either haven't done this for very long, or you've been spectacularly lucky.

This is when the slashing starts. You have to get rid of enough features to make it possible to ship your new payment system in something approaching a reasonable amount of time.

Of course, the designer is all done with this project and on to the next one. This means that the product manager and the engineers are in charge of changing the interface to remove features.

The problem is that, when you remove features, it can change flows and layouts and errors and user stories and all sorts of other things that your designer probably worked on. If you slash enough, you're going to need to bring the designer back in to redo screens and flows. This causes a delay, which in turn means that you've got an engineering team sitting around waiting to start the project.

By the time you actually get the thing built and shipped, it can be months later. The designer is annoyed because you cut half her work. The product manager is annoyed because the feature is missing critical things. The engineers are annoyed because they had to sit around waiting for things and then were forced to work overtime when they finally got the specs.

But worst of all, the users are totally indifferent. The payment method has absolutely no effect on revenue.

When you've spent months working on a particular feature, and then nobody cares about it, it's a tremendous hit to morale. Killing it is tough because so many people have spent so much time on it. Iterating on it is unlikely to work because you have to go through the same process you originally went through that turned out something terrible. Basically, you've just wasted thousands of hours, and you have something that nobody wants.

The Cross-Functional Team

Instead, let's look at how this might work with a Lean, cross-functional team.

Rather than the product manager going off to think of how the feature will work on her own, the product owner will likely explain the metric that she wants to improve. If they don't already know the issues that are causing the metric to be low—let's say in this case it's revenue—she'll run some quick user research to find some likely problems or opportunities for improvements. The designer should be intimately involved with this research, and engineers should attend at least a few research sessions to stay in touch with the customers, of course.

Once they understand the problems, the team will work together to identify a project that they think will have a good ROI. By involving product, design, and engineering at this point, the team will be able to more quickly assess the likely costs of the various projects. They might decide to create a new payment flow, as the first team did, or they might find some alternate option that takes less time but is just as likely to improve things.

After they decide, the team will come up with the minimum set of features needed to run the experiment. See the chapter on MVPs to understand this better. The idea here though, is that the product owner and the designer aren't going to go off and design the biggest possible version of the feature. They'll spend time figuring out what the smallest thing they can build is that will validate their hypothesis.

The next step is to get everybody working on their parts of the project. Typically, this means that the designer and product owner start working on things like sketches and prototypes (see most of the rest of the book for tips on this), while the engineering team begins building.

What's this? How can the engineers start building things before they know exactly what to build? Well, in my experience, there are almost always lots of things that engineers can get started building before they have final screens. In the case of a new payment flow, there will likely be new payment-provider integrations or security issues to address.

Meanwhile, once the designer has sketches or prototypes in a state that she feels comfortable with (this should be days, not weeks), she can have the engineers start working on those.

Now, don't forget, in many cases, this will involve prototype testing. I've found that it's a good idea to have the engineers involved in the prototype-testing process so that they can see users interacting with the feature they're about to build. It gives them a much better sense for how the feature is supposed to behave and helps the whole team understand corner cases and possible errors.

Possibly the most important thing is that the whole team is involved with monitoring and responding to the user behavior. This means that, as soon as the feature is launched and the team starts getting feedback, the entire team can respond and iterate.

If there are bug reports, the team can quickly prioritize and address them. If there is no significant improvement in the targeted metric, the team can connect with users to understand what went wrong. Regardless of what happens, the team can easily begin iterating on the feature, building out parts of it that weren't addressed in the initial work.

By creating a cross-functional team that is responsible for a metric, the company suddenly becomes more flexible and more able to respond quickly to feedback and changes in strategy. This is especially critical for startups, which always need to be ready to pivot.

The reason this works is that everybody is working on the same thing at the same time, which means that there are no handoffs where information gets garbled or lost. Problems, whether technical or design related, are found earlier because everybody is looking at the same things and learning from the same users. It also builds trust among the various groups so that people quickly learn to work together as one team rather than as a sequence of smaller, sometimes antagonistic, teams.

Combine Product and UX Roles

This particular tip is more suited to very small companies, so if you're applying Lean Startup to a large organization, you may be able to safely ignore this one.

In most big companies, the product manager or owner role is quite separate from the product or interaction design role. The jobs are specifically set up so that the product owner does things like gathering information about the users, creating specifications for the product, and managing the engineering team as they write the code.

At a startup where the engineering team consists of fewer than seven or eight engineers, often this becomes far more product overhead than is truly necessary. There simply isn't enough work to support two people in this role.

By combining the two roles into one person, you end up with a single individual in charge of gathering information about the user, translating that information into well-designed features, and then following up with the engineering department to make sure that the features are implemented correctly.

On a very small team, this can be a fantastic way to reduce overhead, save money, and move faster.

Avoid Engineering When Possible

One of the most important things I've learned to do in Lean UX is to avoid engineering whenever possible. This isn't because of some barely repressed hatred of engineers. Well, not entirely, anyway. It's because engineers are expensive and busy.

If the driving force behind the Lean methodology is to always treat everything as a hypothesis to be validated, then the goal here is to see how much validation you can do before writing any code or building any products.

Interactive prototypes can be a way to validate hypotheses, but they are only one in a long list of ways to avoid engineers.

Let me give you an example. One company I worked with sold children's clothing. They wanted to test a feature that allowed their users to preorder merchandise before they committed to having it made in order to help them figure out how many of each item they should order.

Building the feature would have involved quite a lot of work for the engineers. Before we set them to work getting the feature built, we decided to test the two riskiest hypotheses—whether people would preorder a piece of children's clothing and what we would need to offer them to get enough people to buy.

Instead of building the feature into the site, we selected one jacket that was not yet available in the store and promoted it as a preorder on the blog and in our email newsletter. We allowed people to fill out a form saying they wanted the jacket and to pay for it using PayPal. Total engineering time was roughly five minutes to get the PayPal button hooked up.

We then started taking preorders on the jacket and compared the conversion rates to the conversion rates on actual products that we promoted in a similar way.

Was this a perfect representation of exactly how many people would make a preorder if the feature were integrated into the site itself? No. In fact, it was probably a conservative estimate. However, the fact that we could get people to preorder jackets using nothing but the blog and a PayPal button was a great indication that this was a good feature.

The great thing about tests like this is that they are incredibly easy to iterate on. While engineering was building the basic preorder functionality into the site, we could continue to test things like how far in advance people would preorder items, how much of a discount was enough to get people to preorder, and what sorts of products converted best.

The other great thing about tests like this is that they are practically free to run.

Loosely Related Rant: Ship It Already! Just Not to Everyone at Once

There is a pretty common fear that people have. They're concerned that if they ship something that isn't ready, they'll get hammered and lose all their customers. Startups that have spent many painstaking months acquiring a small group of loyal customers are hesitant to lose those customers by shipping something bad.

I get it. It's scary. Sorry, cupcake. Do it anyway.

First, your early adopters tend to be much more forgiving of a few misfires. They're used to it. They're early adopters. Yours is likely not the first product they've adopted early. If you're feeling uncomfortable, go to the Wayback Machine (*http://web.archive.org/*) and look at some first versions of products you use every day. When your eyes stop bleeding, come back and finish this book. I'll wait.

Still nervous? That's OK. The lucky thing is that you don't have to ship your ridiculous first draft of a feature to absolutely everybody at once. Let's look at a few strategies you can use to reduce the risk.

The Interactive Prototype

A prototype is the lowest risk way you can get your big change, new feature, or possible pivot in front of real users without ruining your existing product. Yes. Prototypes can count as shipping. If you're getting something you've created in front of users and learning from it, that's the most important thing. And you'd be surprised at how often prototypes can help you find easy-to-fix problems before you ever write a line of "real code."

If you don't want to build an entire interactive prototype, try showing mockups, sketches, or wireframes of what you're considering. The trick is that you have to show it to your real, current users.

For more info on what sort of prototype is right for you, read Chapter 8. For more info on research, read the whole first half of the book.

If your product involves any sort of user-generated content, taking the time to include some of the tester's own content can be extremely helpful. For example, if it's a marketplace where you can buy and sell handmade stuff, having the user's own items can make a mockup seem more familiar and orient the user more quickly.

Of course, if there's sensitive financial data or anything private, make sure to get the user's permission *before* you include that info in their interactive prototype. Otherwise, it's just creepy.

The Opt In

Another method that works well is the opt in. While early adopters tend to be somewhat forgiving of changes or new features, people who opt in to those changes are even more so.

Allowing people to opt in to new features means that you have a whole group of people who are not only accepting of change but actively seeking it out. That's great for getting very early feedback while avoiding the occasional freakout from the small percentage of people who just enjoy screaming, "Things were better before!"

Here's a fun thing you can learn from your opt-in group: If people who explicitly ask to see your new feature hate your new feature, your new feature probably sucks.

The Opt Out

Of course, you don't want to test your new features or changes only with people who are excited about change. You also want to test them with people who hate change, since they're the ones who are going to scream loudest.

Once you're pretty sure that your feature doesn't suck, you can share it with more people. Just make sure to let them go back to the old way, and then measure the number of people who actually do switch back.

Is it a very vocal 1% that is voting with their opt out? You're probably OK. Is half of your user base switching back in disgust? You may not have nailed that whole "making it not suck" thing.

The n% Rollout

Even with an opt out, if you've got a big enough user base, you can still limit the percentage of users who see the change. In fact, you really should be split testing this thing 50/50, but if you want to start with just 10% to make sure you don't have any major surprises, that's a totally reasonable thing to do.

When you roll a new feature out to a small percentage of your users, just make sure that you know what sorts of things you're looking for. This is a great strategy for seeing if your servers are going to keel over, for example.

It's also nice for seeing if that small, randomly selected cohort behaves any differently from the group that doesn't have the new feature. Is that cohort more likely to make a purchase? Are they more likely to set fire to their computers and swear never to use your terrible product ever again? These are both good things to know.

Do remember, however, that people on the Internet talk about things. Kind of a lot. If you have any way at all for your users to be in contact with one another, people will find out that their friends are seeing something different. This can work for or against you.

Just figure out who's whining the loudest about being jealous of the other group, and you'll know whether to continue the rollout. What you want to hear is, "Why don't I have New New New New New Thing yet?" and not "Just be thankful that they haven't forced the hideous abomination on you. Then you will have to set your computer on fire."

The New User Rollout

Of course, if you're absolutely terrified of your current user base (and you'd be surprised at how many startups seem to be), you can always release the change only to new users.

This is nice, because you get two completely fresh cohorts where the only difference is whether or not they've seen the change. It's a great way to do A/B testing.

On the other hand, if it's something that's supposed to improve things for retained users or users with lots of data, it can take a really long time to get enough information from this. After all, you need those new cohorts to turn into retained users before seeing any actual results, and that can take months.

Also, whether or not new users love your changes doesn't always predict whether your old users will complain. Your power users may have invested a lot of time and energy into setting up your product just the way they want it, and making major changes that are better for new folks doesn't always make them very happy.

In the end, you need to make the decision whether you'll have enough happy new users to offset the possibly angry old ones. But you'll probably need to make that decision about a million more times in the life of your startup, so get used to it.

So are you ready to ship it, already? Yes. Yes, you are. Just don't ship it to everybody all it once.

Go Do This Now!

- Get rid of the waterfall: Try creating small, cross-functional teams that are each responsible for a single metric.

- Ship it to 1%: Try building the functionality that will allow you to do partial rollouts of your features so that you can easily control how many people see each feature.

- Pair up: If you have both product managers and designers on a team, try having them work as pairs, so that they can each learn from the other and share critical user knowledge.

CHAPTER 13

The Big Finish

Congratulations! You made it through the whole book!

Or maybe you just skipped directly to the end, to see if I could summarize it all in a few pithy paragraphs. If so, your laziness has paid off.

If you get nothing else from this book, please remember these three key points:

User research

Listen to your users. All the time. I mean it.

Validation

When you make assumptions or create hypotheses, test them before spending lots of time building products around them.

Design

Iterate. Iterate. Iterate.

That's it. That's all I've got. Good luck to you. Ship something amazing.

If you have follow-up questions or just want to chat about Lean UX, feel free to email me at *laura@usersknow.com*.

Index

W

waterfall method, 187–189
website resources. *See also* tools
    design patterns, 99
    for this book, vii
wireframes, 122–125
    tools for, 125
    when to use, 124–125
Wizard of Oz features, 90–91

Y

Yoskovitz, Ben (author)
    Lean Analytics, 52

About the Author

Laura Klein has spent 15 years as an engineer and designer. Her goal is to help Lean Startups learn more about their customers so that they can build better products faster.

Her popular design blog, *Users Know* (*http://usersknow.blogspot.com/*), teaches product owners exactly what they need to know to do just enough research and design.